HOUSES WITHOUT NAMES

HOUSES WITHOUT NAMES

Architectural Nomenclature and the
Classification of America's Common Houses

Thomas C. Hubka

Vernacular Architecture Studies
Thomas Carter and Anna Vemer Andrzejewski, Series Editors

THE UNIVERSITY OF TENNESSEE PRESS / KNOXVILLE

 The Vernacular Architecture Studies Series provides focused investigations into methodological and theoretical issues in the field of vernacular architecture studies. Written by experts in the field with the student, practitioner, and general public in mind, the series will comprise handbooks and historically grounded instructional texts that embody the very latest research from a burgeoning discipline in an accessible, practical form.

Copyright © 2013 by The University of Tennessee Press / Knoxville.
All Rights Reserved. Manufactured in the United States of America.
First Edition.

The paper in this book meets the requirements of American National Standards Institute / National Information Standards Organization specification Z39.48-1992 (Permanence of Paper). It contains 30 percent post-consumer waste and is certified by the Forest Stewardship Council.

Library of Congress Cataloging-in-Publication Data

Hubka, Thomas C., 1946–
Houses without names: architectural nomenclature and the classification of America's common houses / Thomas C. Hubka. — First [edition].
       pages cm. — (Vernacular architecture studies)
Includes bibliographical references and index.
ISBN 978-1-57233-947-7 (pbk.) — ISBN 1-57233-947-0 (paperback)
1. Architecture, Domestic—United States—Classification.
2. Vernacular architecture—United States—Classification.
3. Architecture and society—United States.
I. Title.

NA7205.H76 2013
728.0973—dc23

2013001554

Contents

Foreword　vii
Preface　ix

1 | Houses without Names: The Problem of Interpreting America's Common Houses　1

2 | Underlying Themes for Understanding Common Houses　31

3 | Emphasizing the Floor Plan in Common Houses　47

4 | Identifying the Floor Plan from the Outside　69

5 | Houses with Names: Interpreting America's Common Houses　83

Notes　95
Index　109

Foreword

As the saying goes "sometimes you get what you ask for," and this seems the case in vernacular architecture studies: our success in making common buildings an acceptable part of what architectural and preservation historians do has created a crisis in the area of nomenclature. By arguing for an inclusive approach to the built environment, one that considers all buildings, big and small, plain and fancy, high and low, we now have hundreds and hundreds of new building types of all kinds to consider—and name! What do we call them? Some houses like the *bungalow* and *ranch* have names, but the majority do not. Yet naming such buildings remains important as a means of understanding them, talking about them with others, determining their significance, and giving them legitimacy. It's a simple matter of respect.

Much work has been done in the area of vernacular architecture nomenclature. Scanning the pages of the Vernacular Architecture Forum's journal, *Perspectives in Vernacular Architecture* (now *Buildings and Landscapes*), we encounter many attempts to bring new building types into the discourse, and part of this has involved naming. Most of this work has been on the pre-industrial side of things, so we have names for these buildings. We are on shakier ground when we try to account for the surge in construction ushered in by industrialization and mass production in the building trades. Beginning after the Civil War and running into the present, we see a proliferation of new building types, and particularly houses. While aspects of this history have received attention, there is no agreed-upon nomenclature or system by which we can explain the diversity of these buildings, which account for a high percentage of America's common housing. It is this group of newcomers that Tom Hubka's book, *Houses without Names*, addresses. Professor Hubka offers not a set of names, but rather a *system* for naming based on distinctive internal (plan) and external (form) characteristics. Further, his naming model is grounded in local production and variation, and accurately concludes that the best and most reliable names will be generated from systematic surveys of existing examples, not arbitrarily applied from the outside.

It is with pleasure therefore that we welcome this book into the Vernacular Architecture Forum's special series. This is the second book in the series, following *Invitation to Vernacular Architecture: A Guide to the Study of Vernacular Buildings and Landscapes* (2005). This new offering meets a real need in our field, which is to address the problem of nomenclature. If we are to have a "new" architectural history, one that includes common buildings, then we do have to know what to call them. We owe them this much.

Anna Andrzejewski
University of Wisconsin–Madison

Thomas Carter
University of Utah

Series Editors

Preface

This book was written in appreciation of common houses. These are the kind of houses you might pass every day but probably escape your attention. Usually these dwellings have only general names if they have any names at all. So you might call them common, popular, vernacular, average, developer-built, middle- or working-class, ordinary, tract, speculative, everyday houses. Whatever you call them, they constitute the largest portion of American housing in all regions and historic periods. Here we propose ways to name and classify them as a way of understanding and appreciating them.

This book is the second in a Vernacular Architecture Study series sponsored by the Vernacular Architecture Forum (VAF). The first book, *Invitation to Vernacular Architecture* by Thomas Carter and Elizabeth Collins Cromley, is a foundational study of research methods to which this more specific study is a direct continuation. To emphasize this relationship, basic definitions and concepts from *Invitation to Vernacular Architecture* will be frequently cited. The series was created to provide focused methodological and theoretical investigations intended for a wide audience including students, practitioners, and the general public. Consequently, this book about common dwellings is addressed to housing professionals, including preservationists, academics, and architects, as well as owners and residents of common houses and anyone interested in housing. Because of this wide audience and the likelihood that some chapters might be read separately or in part, each chapter includes a short summary of previously developed themes. To promote understanding by different types of readers, there are numerous diagrams and illustrations with extensive captions in what might be labeled a *National Geographic* style to encourage quick surveying as well as an aid to more careful reading.

Others have tried different approaches to the difficult problem of housing interpretation and classification, including, most notably, Herbert Gottfried and Jan Jennings, *American Vernacular Buildings and Interiors*; Christine Hunter, *Ranches, Rowhouses, and Railroad Flats*; Daniel D. Reiff, *Houses from Books: Treatises, Pattern Books, and Catalogs in American Architecture, 1738-1950*; Alan Gowans, *The Comfortable House*; John Jakle et al., *Common Houses in America's Small Towns*; Virginia and Lee McAlester, *A Field Guide to American Houses*; Peter G. Rowe, *Making a Middle Landscape*; and Gerald Foster, *American Houses: A Field Guide to the Architecture of the Home*. This work differs from these books principally by maintaining the egalitarian goal of including all houses, especially the most common—a standard often implied but rarely realized.

Because there is so little agreement about what to call and how to classify most common houses (on both national and local levels), I apologize for the names I have inevitably had to select. While I will emphasize the importance of local and regional traditions to formulate names for houses, it is still essential to recognize the vast national unity among common houses that necessitates some form of shared vocabulary. But an apology might still be necessary because, regardless of whether you know a great deal about these houses, local names and terminology have strong staying powers, even if current labels might be shown to be inadequate or confusing. But these are the standard problems of common-house interpretation.

All authors are indebted to the work of previous scholars, this author more than most. I owe debts to Henry Glassie, Leo Marx, Elliot Wolfson, Gwendolyn Wright, Thomas Paine, Dell Upton, Tom Carter, and Elizabeth Cromely. Many people have given their advice and have shaped the development of this book, including Howard Davis, Judith Kenny, Claire Dempsey, Pam Simpson, Kim Hoagland, Chris Wilson, Barbara Wyatt, Kingston Heath, Dell Upton, Art Goldhammer, Catherine Bishir, Carl Lounsbury, Todd Gish, and especially, editors Anna Andrzejewski, Tom Carter, and Scot Danforth.

Many housing specialists and historians from around the country have assisted as local and regional consultants. Many of my students have contributed to this study with their housing investigations, including Shannon Honl, Daniel O'Grady, and especially Scott Mackinson who assisted with the drawings. More difficult to thank are the hundreds of local residents who have answered my questions about their residences and in many cases allowed me to visit their homes.

Special thanks to my Mom, who taught me how to look closely and carefully at things, and to Judith, sophisticated house analyzer and survey car buddy.

1

Houses without Names: The Problem of Interpreting America's Common Houses

For over ten years I have traveled throughout the country, studying America's housing. I have observed hundreds of thousands of houses, most without names. It takes a certain kind of persistence to maintain a sharp focus while surveying thousands of miles of residential streets, but a few moments of inspiration stand out. I particularly remember a residential street in West Allis, Wisconsin, that I saw while conducting a research tour in the town's working-class neighborhoods (fig. 1). One of the tour participants reacting to yet another street lined with small, variegated houses, blurted out, "Why, they're just like a bunch of little bald-headed step-children!" There was laughter, but my students also knew that a line between humor and disrespect had been crossed. Later, as if galvanized by the experience, our group became even more determined to find meaningful names and classification for these step-houses. It is in that spirit I stress the importance of housing nomenclature, not as a matter of sympathy for these nameless houses, but to recognize their role in the development of American domestic culture and its housing landscape.

Fig. 1. Working-class bungalows (bungalow plans), West Allis, Wisconsin.

Eighty Million Houses

There are approximately 80 million houses and housing structures (containing 130 million households) in the United States today.[1] The vast majority have only loosely fitting, general names, like *ranch, duplex, bungalow, apartment, Cape,* and *flat.* Most houses, however, cannot even be identified by such common names, much less by an architectural style, such as *Colonial, Italianate,* or *Queen Anne,* terms that have long been used as the standard for housing classification. Furthermore, while a few vernacular houses, like the split-level, shotgun, Cape (Cod), and three-decker, have received scholarly attention and are regionally recognized, these houses are the exceptions, not the rule (fig. 2). Far more typical are houses that are only loosely named and rarely analyzed or classified with any degree of accuracy. To illustrate some of these basic problems, figure 3 shows many difficult-to-identify single- and multi-family common houses from different historical periods and various regions of the country. (For the sake

Fig. 2. Widely recognized house types. (A) Three-decker (various one-story, bungalow plans), Worcester, Massachusetts; (B) Split-level (plan), Union, New Jersey; (C) shotgun houses (shotgun plans), Atlanta, Georgia; (D) Four-square (plan), Portland, Oregon.

(A)

(B)

(C)

(D)

of simplicity, I will concentrate on single-family housing although most of my ideas and recommendations apply to both single- and multi-unit residences.) Most of the houses in this book have been built hundreds of thousands of times in various regional forms and subtypes, yet they have received little historical or interpretive analysis. The vast majority have only generalized local or regional names, imprecise or misleading names or, more typically, no names or meaningful classification at all.

Naming and classifying are ways to better understand common houses. And with greater understanding might come greater appreciation. For many, the appreciation of small common houses may seem particularly far fetched. Yet even the goal of greater understanding might seem inflated because, one might ask, what is there to understand about such simple, obvious, workaday houses? But interpretation and classification are surprisingly difficult goals for a subject that is unexpectedly complex while simultaneously familiar and ordinary.

This book challenges the current ways we see and interpret the common, everyday houses that surround us. Repeatedly, a thin veneer of generally workable terms and interpretations will be shown to conceal a more meaningful story about our housing and its domestic culture (both past and present). Once we begin to see the surprising diversity and depth of traditions disguised under the surface unity of popular housing, we can better appreciate the role that the common residential landscape has played in the larger story of American domestic culture.

To better interpret a common house, a basic naming and classification strategy should combine both exterior and interior terms. This recommendation unites current traditions of exterior facade nomenclature (Queen Anne, ranch style, and side-gable) with less-frequently used interior floor-plan nomenclature (hall-and-parlor, four-square, and two-up and two-down). For basic naming purposes or for more complex analysis, the combination of both exterior and interior classification can bring greater clarity and depth to the overall interpretation. The simple formula of combining an exterior photo and an interior floor plan, as for example in Tom Carter and Peter Goss's *Utah's Historic Architecture, 1847–1940*, brings uncommon clarity to a typically unwieldy popular housing survey.

Because most current house names and classification systems emphasize the external features of a house (either its architectural style or its physical form), a considerable portion of this book emphasizes the internal features of a house (either its floor plan or room usage) in order

4 | HOUSES WITHOUT NAMES

Fig. 3. Difficult-to-identify single-family houses (pages 4–5, A–H): (A) Portland, Oregon; (B) Omaha, Nebraska; (C) Portland, Oregon; (D) Butte, Montana; (E) Portland, Oregon; (F) Milwaukee, Wisconsin; (G) Portland, Oregon; (H) Portland, Oregon. Difficult to identify multi-family or multi-unit houses (pages 5–6, I–P): (I) Milwaukee, Wisconsin; (J) Shorewood, Wisconsin; (K) Shorewood, Wisconsin; (L) Springfield, Oregon; (M) Cincinnati, Ohio; (N) Boston, Massachusetts; (O) Portland, Oregon; (P) Cincinnati, Ohio.

HOUSES WITHOUT NAMES | 5

(G)

(H)

(I)

(J)

(K)

(L)

(M)

(N)

(O)

(P)

to achieve a balanced interpretation of inside and out. Despite the need for new kinds of names, I do not generally advocate major changes to current housing nomenclature and classification categories, especially well-known names, like *shotgun, ranch,* and *bungalow.* Most current names are reasonably sufficient, although they are most often too general and need to be clarified and refocused, usually to acknowledge the disguised variations of interior floor plans. In the case of the smallest, most popular houses, however, those lacking in all but the most generic classification, new names and classification will be suggested.

Common Houses

There is a vast quantity of housing about which there are few agreed-upon terms, definitions, or boundaries. Although I will interchange the terms *popular, vernacular, average, ordinary,* and *everyday* to describe the same houses, *common* is the term that best conveys the essential ideas. (For this and other vernacular definitions, I follow *Invitation to Vernacular Archi-*

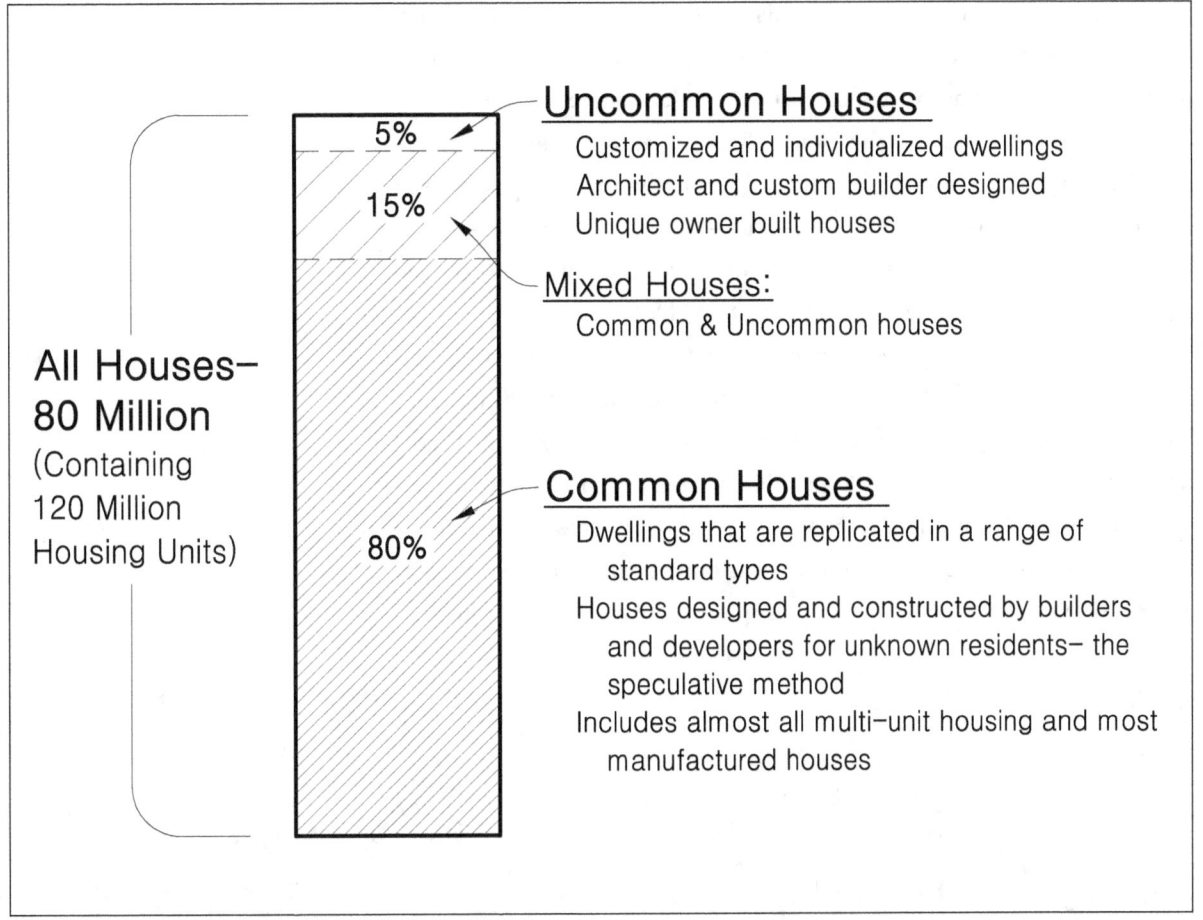

Fig. 4. Common and uncommon houses. The number of builder/developer-produced common houses compared to the number of architect/custom-builder-produced uncommon houses for individual owners.

tecture, henceforth *IVA*, 7–13.)[2] While the word *common* is imprecise, the central core of dwellings I seek to interpret is clear and massive—more than three-fourths of current and historic American housing, or over 60 million of the current 80 million houses, with increasing percentages in earlier periods (fig. 4). These "common houses" include most small-to-medium-sized houses (and almost all multi-unit houses) that were not designed and constructed by architects and builders for individual owners. This great body of common dwellings is readily recognized by their most popular national types, including ranches, Capes, and bungalows (fig. 5). Because estimates of the most popular, numerous "common houses" are usually based on currently existing houses, most estimates reflect the greater numbers of post–World War II housing units and diminish the relative importance of the most popular houses in previous periods. Ideally, common houses could be classified by census estimates in previous historic periods, but this type of information gathering is not currently available.[3]

Houses not included under this broad label, *common,* principally include an upper- and upper-middle class of high-style or elite dwellings usually designed by architects or custom builders and characterized by increasing levels of individualization and customization in exterior styles and interior plans. While a large body of dwellings with varying degrees of customized and non-customized (speculative) design exists between these two major categories (see fig. 4), the fundamental distinction between common and uncommon dwellings is substantial.[4]

The term *common* also follows Eric Mercer's definition in *English Vernacular Architecture* where "vernacular architecture is the common buildings of a particular place and time," and the buildings that most people build and use (*IVA,* 8). Expanding on this traditional definition, I will emphasize the occurrence of similar common houses in great numbers. This expanded emphasis, however, is one of the most controversial aspects of common housing—their multiple, repetitive character in large

(A)

(B)

(C)

Fig. 5. Three of America's most popular common-house types. Although generally recognizable in most areas of the country, each type was built in distinct regional varieties and subtypes: (A) bungalow (bungalow plan), Portland, Oregon; (B) Cape (no uniform name, expanded four-box plan), Milwaukee, Wisconsin; (C) ranch (ranch plan), Portland, Oregon.

numbers (fig. 6). This standard critique of "mass culture" repetition has a long history in art and architecture scholarship but intensified during the late nineteenth century in reaction to the industrial standardization that produced the vast majority of America's common houses. Despite this criticism, understanding the repetitive nature of common houses' production is essential to interpreting their strategic place in the creation of America's residential landscapes and its domestic culture. For example, it is important to recognize that most common houses have been built hundreds of thousands, and in several cases, millions of times. Yet rather than interpreting this characteristic entirely as a negative, uniformity on this scale can also be interpreted as an indication of the shared values underlying the selection of particular house types and floor plans for their builders and users. While acknowledging this unity, it is also essential to recognize the many unanticipated variations and differences among these common repetitive houses (typically unobserved by critics), producing standard

(A)

(B)

(C)

Fig. 6. Repetition in common houses: (A) Two-up and two-down, Pittsburgh, Pennsylvania; (B) side-hall (plan), row houses, Butte, Montana; (C) Capes (no uniform name), West Allis, Wisconsin.

subtypes as well as considerable local and regional variation, especially in comparison to seemingly uniform national types.

Although the process has not been well studied, the way common houses have typically been designed and built tells us a great deal about these structures. Their modern-vernacular method of construction and development—the speculative building process—is the system by which local builders and developers produced dwellings for unknown clients or users (see chapter 2 and *IVA*, 13–18). Although widely maligned in professional and popular literature, the practice of repetitive-speculative development is by far the most dominant method of construction for well over three-fourths of America's housing units today and in most regions since the late nineteenth century.[5]

These millions of repetitive and speculatively built common houses can seldom be compared or analyzed, much less classified, with any degree of accuracy. And while differentiating houses by name is only a minimal, basic step in a larger material-culture interpretive process, naming is, nevertheless, an indispensable component to understanding and appreciation. For to name is to award basic recognition where today only a jumble of generalized, often misleading terms inhibits the recognition of underlying patterns of organization that could provide a basis for meaningful interpretation. This lack of interpretive nomenclature has in no small measure guaranteed that the bulk of common houses is poorly understood, marginalized, and predictably ignored.

Current Practices for Classification and Naming

To those familiar with the vast literature of housing, this claim of anonymity and neglect might seem exaggerated. There is a considerable body of work on many types of housing, including vernacular houses. Scholars associated with the Vernacular Architecture Forum have produced hundreds of books and articles on vernacular housing, including many articles in *Perspectives in Vernacular Architecture*. Furthermore, there are wide-ranging studies of the most dominant types of vernacular housing, like the bungalow and ranch, as well as detailed studies of particular, regional forms of common housing, such as the three-decker, shotgun, Cape Cod, Polish flat, Baltimore row house, and New England connected farm.[6]

Yet despite the strength of many individual works, these studies still represent only a thin, patchwork sampling of the most readily identifiable house types within a much larger volume of truly anonymous and difficult-to-classify common houses (see figs. 4 and 5). This lack of demographic comprehensiveness has contributed to our current haphazard traditions of popular-housing identification. When coupled with a professional vocabulary based on exterior stylistic classification derived from larger elite houses, it is not surprising that common housing has remained understudied and underappreciated. Furthermore, these current practices actually contribute to concealing the external variety and especially the internal organization that can actually form the basis for meaningful interpretation and classification.

Of course, this lack of study does not mean that we know little about these houses or are unable to converse about them. Typically, however, our personal knowledge is confined to a very small sample of the whole, and this limitation is a significant detriment to understanding the problems of housing identification. For example, in everyday conversation, most people maintain a simple, abbreviated vocabulary about housing to get around a general lack of specific names and categories. These basic terms, such as *house, home, place, farm, block,* and *unit,* constitute a flexible generic vocabulary for identification. We may add positive terms like *palace, mansion, pad, loft, country house*; or negative terms, perhaps to identify other people's houses, such as *tract house, developer spec, flat, trailer,* and *shack.* From experience or training, we may also employ generally accepted terms such as *ranch, duplex, bungalow,* and *apartment block.* Or we may use more specific, local, and regional names such as *pyramid, two-flat, Georgian, cube, six-pack, three-decker, Cape, mill cottage, ding-bat,* and *two-up and two-down.* Or we may even use names from a more precise, professional vocabulary of architectural styles such as *Queen Anne, Romanesque,* and *Dutch Colonial*—terms often employed by housing professionals and academics. Unfortunately, this professional vocabulary of stylistic terminology can seldom be stretched to apply to most common housing, and it is a major impediment to awarding names and meaningful classification to houses without names.

Thus our popular perception and understanding of housing is limited, but it is also facilitated by a highly influential real-estate and housing-development industry. For example, real-estate listings, especially influential to housing classification, combine many types of names in useful, flattering, but highly irregular patterns of naming and categorization that are only broadly accurate, and often purposely or naively misleading. But in several crucial ways, this abbreviated language of the real-estate agent, as condensed throughout the country in short listings, does provide a potential basis for housing nomenclature and classification by means of room-function analysis. When a house is described as a two-bedroom, one-and-one-half bath with one-car garage and unfinished basement, most people have received enough significant information to begin to form a basic understanding of this type of house. There are limits to this kind of classification, especially because there are many very different kinds of houses that can be described in the same way. Nevertheless, this room-usage, functional vocabulary is the vehicle by which most common-house users understand popular housing types, and this functional vocabulary can be used to reconfigure a much more useful nomenclature and classification of popular housing.

CURRENT NAMES FOR COMMON HOUSES

When viewed as a whole, the current names for common houses reveal the confusing, non-hierarchal, non-historical nature of the interpretive process. It is a free-market evolution of a few older "historic" names, such as *bungalow, garrison,* and *Georgian,* vying with new labels, such as *narrow-lot ranch* and *tri-plex,* derived from a variety of professional and academic sources, including architectural historians, architects, builders, and realtors, and mixed together in popular usage. It is a diverse parentage demonstrating both cultural synthesis and serendipity. With such an uneven tradition of labeling, it is no wonder that most current efforts to bring interpretive order become mired in confusing names and categories. The chart below (fig. 7) outlines some of the variegated sources for the names of common housing.

Adding to the dilemma of vernacular nomenclature, many names for common houses were not known to their original occupants or even used during their original period of development. Most names, such as *garrison, four-square,* and *Cape Cod,* are labels applied in later periods by historians, preservationists, and local observers. (Popular original names like *ranch, split-level,* and *bungalow* are conspicuous exceptions to this general rule.) Furthermore, many of the names coined by academics and housing professionals, like *I-house, period revival,* and *hall-and-parlor,* are not popularly used or generally understood by current residents and the general public, thus further complicating the identification and classification process.[7]

Fig 7. NAMES FOR COMMON HOUSES

MAJOR CATEGORIES & EXAMPLES

Many house names, like bungalow and hall-and-parlor, have multiple, overlapping meanings which combine style, form, and plan characteristics.

Architectural Style: For example: Greek revival, prairie style, Italianate, Queen Anne, Second Empire, Tudor, period revival, bungalow, craftsman, modern, Colonial, stick style, ranch (style), Georgian, etc.

Massing/Exterior Form: For example: Temple-and-wing, dog trot, octagon, three-decker, cross-gable, camel back, box-ranch, Gambrel/Mansard, cottage, I-house, side-gable, garrison, pyramid, shed, multi-gable (style), etc.

Floor Plan: For example: Four-square, side-hall, split-level, split entry, double pile, center-stair, hall-and-parlor, ranch (plan), two-up and two-down, Georgian (plan), bungalow (plan), four-box, Cape Cod (plan), etc.

SECONDARY SOURCES FOR NAMES

There are many regional terms and local variations of the following names.

Ownership/Rental Type: Single-family, four-plex, two-flat, six-pack, duplex, row house, town house, walk-up, condominium/condo, tenement, motel type, etc.

Material/Structural System: Adobe, geodesic dome, wood frame, log house, balloon-frame, A-frame, concrete block house, etc.

Geographic Context/Historical Source: California bungalow, Cape Cod, Midwest-cube, Baltimore row house, suburban ranch, New England connected farm, Chicago bungalow, etc.

Ethnic Group/User: Polish flat, Dutch colonial, Belgian farm house, workers' cottage, Irish cottage, German farm house, etc.

Historic/Multi-Sources: shotgun, cottage, tenement, flat, ranch, vernacular, storybook, bungalow, telescope, etc.

Positive & Negative Images: mansion, McMansion, tenement, townhouse, trailer, palace, flat, developer ranch, loft, snout-house, "spec" house, etc.

Yet despite this confusing background, the outlines of meaningful reform are clearly discernable. Many current names, such as *ranch, split-level,* and *bungalow,* are generally accurate and popularly understood. Typically, however, these names are applied too broadly and require adjustment to address a wide range of unrecognized or poorly understood subtypes. In many other cases, however, new names adjusted to the subtle variations of local and regional development will be needed for houses that either have no name or, more often, misleading, overlapping, generalized, or ill-fitting names. Such re-evaluation requires careful field study and historic analysis, as well as public consensus-building.

Common Houses and Professional Evaluation

Once the problems of common housing interpretation are explained, most people can generally appreciate the need for an improved classification and nomenclature. For many professionals, however, especially architectural historians, preservationists, and architects, the reform of long-entrenched practices that have excluded or minimized vernacular topics has proven extremely difficult. Despite the considerable recent interest in popular-culture topics such as housing, this interest has generally not translated into meaningful institutional reform of current evaluation systems based primarily on older, elite standards, particularly architectural style. For example, in meetings with the staff of state historical preservation offices, it becomes clear that, despite good vernacular intentions, the dominant stylistic- or historic-integrity evaluative criteria make it extremely difficult to assess or even count, much less to award architectural merit to common houses. When challenged about exclusive criteria, current practices are legitimized as far too difficult to change and the possible rewards of change are just not worth the confusion, inconvenience, and disruption such revisions might cause. Despite the growing support for greater inclusion of vernacular topics, the strength of elite traditions and institutional inertia within professional organizations makes the prospects for greater common housing inclusion a work in progress.

For meaningful academic and professional institutional reform to occur, it will be critically important to revise the criteria by which vernacular buildings are evaluated, classified, and finally named. Yet the necessity and mechanics of nomenclature reform should not overwhelm the larger motivation for greater understanding and appreciation of common houses. We need to identify these millions of modest houses in order to better understand their place and contribution to a larger domestic cultural landscape. It is not that they are invisible, yet surely they are understudied and underappreciated. Borrowing biological imagery, it is almost as if, lacking proper names for common houses, we find ourselves within a dense landscape of unnamed or poorly named houses. Consequently, we are unable to identify the diversity that, once revealed, opens new possibilities for understanding and appreciating the housing and domestic culture of most Americans.

For example, no skilled botanist or nature enthusiast could imagine walking through a forest without the means for identifying, or at least differentiating between, the basic species of plant life—the building blocks of classification and appreciation. Yet when we drive down a typical residential street, we have so few ways to interpret the diversity of common housing, either popularly or academically and professionally. In a forest, we might be satisfied simply by saying that everything is merely shades of green, as we could also say that a typical residential street merely contains a lot of anonymous houses. But in both cases, we would be missing out on hidden worlds of appreciation just beyond our reach. And although nomenclature is not the central issue in either case, no botanist would ever discount the role of naming and classification in the process of species identification and, ultimately, figuring out biological diversity, and, I hope, housing diversity.

While this Darwinian parallel may seem slightly exaggerated for observing a street of common ranch houses, still, in fundamentally similar ways, the collective body of common housing remains underexplored and often misinterpreted. Once we begin to see the diversity in common houses on the streets and in the neighborhoods we know best, we will soon discover, as Darwin certainly discovered in the Galapagos, that local species had unanticipated similarities and differences with species in other places. If we look more closely, we will also discover that, while conforming to larger national types, our local housing also yields unanticipated, unpredictable variations of local form and usage. These variations of the local, as Darwin also recognized, can only be understood through careful local inspection. We are not sailing in Darwin's Beagle, and the residential landscape of common houses outside your door is not the Galapagos. Yet, there are significant parallels you may wish to consider as we voyage into the relatively uncharted waters of your local community's underexplored and almost certainly unnamed common houses.

Historic Traditions of Nomenclature and Classification

Most of the ways we name and classify houses, both common and uncommon, were derived from three principal sources: the architectural style of the exterior, the physical shape or massing of the house, and the floor plan or room function of the interior. These traditional categories provide a starting point for understanding the strength and weaknesses of current practices for naming and classifying common houses.

Classification by Architectural Style

Figure 3 showed many difficult to identify, common houses. But if larger, high-style, "historic" houses were selected, there would not have been a problem of nomenclature. These larger houses do have names—very precise names. They share a highly developed vocabulary of architectural style—a historic system of nomenclature and classification used by architectural historians, architects, preservationists, and housing professionals (fig. 8).

Architectural style is a historic language of building classification based on the evaluation of exterior facade composition and ornamentation through historic periods. It is a system that has proven extremely successful for interpreting and ranking the major types of high-style, architect-designed, public and institutional buildings and upper-class housing for hundreds of years. Classification by historic style had a long period of development in Western Europe, originating in Renaissance attempts to classify and reinterpret a Greek and Roman architectural heritage. This system of Renaissance classicism was greatly expanded in the eighteenth and nineteenth centuries in a period of Enlightenment-inspired scientific classification, first by interpreting the historic development of Western European architecture and later by interpreting and ordering worldwide, multicultural traditions of architectural ornamentation and detail.[8]

In the American development of stylistic classification, English and French traditions of architectural ornamentation were gradually extended to the houses of the middle classes. From the late colonial period and throughout most of the nineteenth century, the language and rules of architectural stylistic ornamentation, the "classical orders," were disseminated in popular builders' pattern books which helped to popularize the application of architectural ornamentation to most buildings.[9] With the spread of architectural ornamentation to middle-class and common

(A)

(B)

(C)

(D)

Fig. 8. Houses classified by architecture style: (A) Gothic style, side-gable (various names, side-gable plan), Eugene, Oregon; (B) Queen Anne style, Victorian/Queen Anne cottage (parlor-by-pass plan), Portland, Oregon; (C) Prairie style/Arts-and-Crafts (four-square plan), Portland, Oregon; (D) Tudor style, (central stair-hall plan), Shorewood, Wisconsin.

houses came the usage of stylistic terms such as *Georgian, Greek Revival, Italianate,* and *Gothic,* which were selectively borrowed and absorbed into the standard vocabulary for the ornamentation and naming of middle-class houses as well as some forms of common houses.

Consequently, we still use the historic language of neoclassical styles (*Georgian, Federal, Greek Revival*) to name and classify many types of late-eighteenth and early nineteenth-century houses including many, but certainly not all, common houses of the late Colonial and early National periods, like popular central-hall and central-chimney, Georgian or Federal (style) houses (fig. 9). Throughout the nineteenth century, the application of consistent patterns of stylistic ornamentation to a wide range of house types produced a set of readily identifiable stylistic facades and floor plans for upper- and middle-class houses with modified applications to smaller, working-class houses. In many regions, these traditional houses

(A)   (B)

Fig. 9. Early nineteenth-century, neo-classical styled houses: (A) center-chimney, Cape Cod (Cape Cod plan); Kennebunk, Maine; (B) Georgian form, I-house (central hall plan), Milton, Pennsylvania.

and their architectural styles continued to be built into the twentieth and twenty-first centuries in modified, Colonial Revival forms (fig. 10). These traditional, one-story Cape Cod houses and two-story Georgian houses are some of the most popular "Colonial Revival" houses to have transitioned through various periods to become popular upper-, middle-, and working-class house types throughout the twentieth century.[10] (Among the many contested traditions of housing nomenclature, none is more complex and contested than what to call modern versions of these Colonial Revival/minimal traditional houses as shown in figure 10.)

Yet, simultaneously, after the middle of the nineteenth century, and increasingly after the Civil War, new materials and techniques of industrialized housing production and new methods of speculative construction and development greatly accelerated the production of new types of houses with new and hybrid types of architectural styles and floor plans. These now-dominant industrialized house types, constructed throughout the country on a massive scale, have generally proven difficult to classify by the historic standards of architectural style or any other method of housing classification (fig. 11). Consequently, throughout the twentieth century, an awkward two-part coexistence of housing classification has generally reigned. Typically a small volume of upper-class houses can be adequately classified by a traditional vocabulary of historic or contemporary styles. Most twentieth-century common houses, however, clad only in partial, irregular, and non-orthodox interpretations of historical styles have received minimum or inadequate interpretation.[11] After more than a century, this basic two-part division of haves and have nots is ripe for reevaluation and change.

(A)

(B)

(C)

Fig. 10. Twentieth-century Colonial-Revival styled houses. (There is little agreement about how to identify these minimally styled "Colonial" detailed, popular houses.) (A) post–World War II, minimal-traditional, "Cape Cod" (various names, expanded four-box plan), Portland, Oregon; (B) gambrel-roof, "Dutch Colonial" (central hall plan), Portland, Oregon; (C) Modern Colonial, with garrison front (side-hall plan), Milwaukee, Wisconsin.

Classification by Exterior Shape, Form, or Massing

During the twentieth century, cultural and vernacular historians, recognizing the limitations of stylistic classification for interpreting common houses, developed taxonomies of exterior volumetric shape or massing, also including some floor-plan analysis. Led by geographers during the middle of the century, classification by exterior shape proved useful for identifying the basic forms of a pre-industrial, typically rural housing, including I-houses, shotguns, cross-gables, saltboxes, dog-trots, and various one-room-deep houses (fig. 12).[12] (The exterior shape of the house is a contributing factor in most systems of housing classification, but the issue here is whether that shape should be the primary factor in analysis. Therefore, a four-square house, described by its four ground-floor rooms in a typically square plan, is also recognized by its boxy exterior shape and its low hip-roof. In the Midwest, the four-square is even called a Midwest-cube, highlighting its exterior shape identification.)

 (A)

 (B)

 (C)

 (D)

Fig. 11. New types of post–Civil War, industrialized houses. (Except for the four-square, these nationally distributed houses have no uniform name.) (A) Four-square (plan), Homestead, Pennsylvania; (B) gable-over-porch form (modified side-hall plan), Portland, Oregon; (C) pyramid (four-box plan), Ashland, Oregon; (D) side-entry, turn-of-the-century cottage (various names, early bungalow plan), Portland, Oregon.

As a broader system of classification, however, exterior shape-form analysis has not proven effective in interpreting the major types of post–Civil War National-era industrialized housing, especially in cities and metropolitan regions where the expression of exterior form is more uniform and constrained. In these environments, as well as many other mainstream twentieth-century residential landscapes, neither massing nor stylistic classification has proven effective in naming and classifying the most common forms of housing.

Classification by Floor Plan

Classifying housing by floor plan has a long history in architectural literature. As part of an Enlightenment quest for scientific classification, the development of floor-plan typologies aided a search for the origins of both classical buildings, like Palladian villas, and vernacular house types, especially the search for their national origins. These European traditions were continued in late-nineteenth and early twentieth-century American stud-

Fig. 12. Houses classified primarily by exterior form and massing: (A) shotgun house (shotgun plan); Macon, Georgia; (B) pyramid (roof, duplex plan), Atlanta, Georgia; (C) I-house (central passage plan), Ashland, Oregon.

ies intended to demonstrate both their European origins and their national development—for example, Isham and Brown's *Early Connecticut Houses*, and continuing in works such as Abbott Lowell Cummings's *The Framed Houses of Massachusetts Bay*, and Dell Upton's "Vernacular Domestic Architecture in Eighteenth-Century Virginia."[13]

Classification by floor plan has been an alternative method for many different types of houses. Floor-plan analysis has been most successfully employed in classifying both pre–Civil War, East Coast English/Georgian housing or the development of individual house types, such as the varieties of the three-decker and the split-level. Less successful have been attempts to interpret floor-plan development for broader segments of post–Civil War American housing, especially the vast production of late-nineteenth and twentieth-century common houses. Where twentieth-century floor-plan classification has been most successfully applied is in the analysis of modern housing developments, especially multi-housing such as high-rise apartment buildings and row housing.[14]

Rarely, however, has plan analysis been successfully applied to the classification of the majority of America's common houses. This book differs from other works on American housing by emphasizing plan classification for all housing, even the most common.[15] Generally, the classification of common housing by floor plan has remained a partial component and circumscribed tradition within housing research and literature. Of the three principal traditions for housing classification—style, form, and plan—the floor plan is probably the least employed in current popular, professional, and academic discourse about common housing.

Myths and Misconceptions about Common Houses

The classification and naming of common houses are only the surface manifestations of a much more complex relationship between housing, residents, and their domestic culture. Because the number of common houses is so large and the range of domestic topics so broad, there are, of course, numerous overlapping and conflicting interpretations about their meaning and significance. Various professional organizations, academic disciplines, and cultural groups all contribute important perspectives, and most of all, everyone seems to have their own opinion about the subject of common housing, especially their own houses.

Beyond the normal push and pull of competing interpretations, however, the subject has been beset by unusually persistent myths, legends, and misinformation. For example, until recently it was rare to find objective, descriptive analysis of common suburban housing, much less the popular housing of previous eras. Consequently many legends and misconceptions about common residential architecture have abounded. These legends might charitably be labeled "urban (or suburban, or rural) myths" but they are hardly benign and have combined in the professional and scholarly literature and especially in popular perception to form a brittle context of misinformation impeding the objective evaluation of common housing, its builders and its residents. It is essential, therefore, to address these persistent myths lest they overwhelm or distort analysis before it begins.

1. Myths of the Rich and Famous

There is abundant research demonstrating our society's fascination with the rich, famous, and special, especially our collective fixation with celebrities and people of wealth and power. One consequence of this collective infatuation is a tendency to emphasize the unique and glamorous and to pay less attention to the ordinary and everyday. Common houses certainly suffer a similar neglect in relation to elaborate one-of-a-kind, architect-designed celebrity mansions. For a variety of reasons, the common houses of everyday life are rarely the subject of sustained, objective investigation, either academically or popularly—they are, perhaps, just too common.

It is not surprising, therefore, that when it comes to assessing common houses, the depth of scholarship influencing popular opinion is predictably thin. Often the focus of media and literature has been drawn to upper-class housing and has generally neglected middle- to working-class housing. The attraction of star-architect-designed houses is well known, but even the current attention given to large suburban mansions or "McMansions" also demonstrates this tendency (fig. 13). Over the last twenty years, in every part of the country, large suburban houses of 3,000 to 6,000 square feet have been continually displayed in media analysis. For every super-sized suburban dwelling, however, three or four times as many smaller, modest housing units have been constructed, including apartments and manufactured homes. These much more numerous "common" houses are rarely the subject of media attention or academic study. Predictably, this repeated focus on elite housing has tended to influence and frame the interpretation of common houses in terms and values that, as we will see, are not always appropriate. In so many ways, we are invited to turn our attention to unique, uncommon houses and to ignore ordinary, common houses.[16]

2. Myths of Suburbia

More than a half-century after the rise of American suburban culture, we still struggle to objectively interpret the suburban residences which today dominate the domestic environment of a majority of Americans. Although these houses have appeared to be mindless "cookie cutter" repetitions to their upper-class commentators since the 1930s, most recent research, while recognizing their many problems, has emphasized the subtle variety of house types and settings within an overall unity of suburban residential landscapes. This "unity," frequently defined as oppressive conformity, is, of course, what is most often criticized (see fig. 6). Yet, in all periods and regions, working- and middle-class American dwellings have consistently maintained an overall uniformity of house types and settings within distinct class-cultural settings.

From the historic perspective of most residents, this conformity probably represented a common-sense expression of the norms of domestic life and certainly not a symptom of communal decline or domestic pathology, as has often been assumed. There is, of course, much to criticize about the development of suburban housing and its domestic culture, especially land and resource waste, racial and class segregation, the abandonment of urban and rural environments and constituencies. Despite these significant critiques, we should still recognize the overwhelming presence of suburban environments and the need for rigorous, objective interpretation. Unfortunately, more than a half-century of sustained critique has made the objective evaluation of suburban housing types, as well as older forms of common housing, much more difficult.[17]

3. Myths of Trickle-Down

The depth and quality of scholarship about high-style, upper-class houses far surpasses that of common houses. On the strength of this scholarship, it is not surprising that ideas and interpretative frameworks derived from the study of upper- to middle-class housing and its domestic culture have consistently been borrowed and applied to the interpretation of average, middle- to working-class housing and households. In the absence of substantive studies, it is often assumed that the builders and residents of

Fig. 13. Late twentieth-century, large suburban housing, or "McMansion" ("great room" plan), Scotch Plains, New Jersey. (There is little agreement about how to identify these nationally distributed houses.)

common houses simply follow the basic building and domestic patterns of upper-class houses and owners. But this trickle-down assumption, that average house builders and users simply imitate high-style leaders, is not confirmed in substantive historical vernacular-housing research. Generally, it is a more balanced two-way relationship of influences, both top-down and bottom-up. (Here I emphasize the bottom-up influence, although common houses are certainly influenced in major ways by high-style and elite architecture.)

Nowhere is this myth of upper-class trickle-down more evident than in the exaggerated influence of late-nineteenth-century Victorian era housing. Based on both the high quality of middle- and upper-class housing studies and the absence of equivalent working-class studies, insights from this literature have unavoidably influenced the account of how common houses were built and inhabited during the late nineteenth and early twentieth century—one of the most critical periods of national, common housing development. For example, typical Victorian era topics such as parlor and back-stair usage, servant control, the usage of space in large kitchens and extra rooms, commuter husbands, free time for wives, new mechanical systems, and exterior architectural style choices for the home have found their way into the perception of common, middle- and working-class housing of the same era. While these culture-of-abundance issues were widely discussed in the elite literature of the era, they had very little to do with the vast majority of working- to middle-class families transitioning from smaller, less-improved to larger, more-improved housing during the same period.

Furthermore, this misapplied middle- to upper-class literature has masked the more essential and difficult-to-articulate issues of common housing development involving both severe constraints and modest advances in housing technologies and domestic usage that typically mark the stages of working- to-middle-class domestic improvement in the second half of the nineteenth and first half of the twentieth centuries. Such improvements are outlined in Joseph Bigott's *From Cottage to Bungalow: Houses and the Working Class in Metropolitan Chicago, 1869-1929*. Unfortunately, by focusing almost exclusively on a vast literature of upper- and upper-middle-class housing, even the best scholarship has tended to either ignore or superimpose elite ideas on the houses and families of the middle and working class during this crucial era of common housing production.[18]

4. Myths of Primordial Origins

One of the traditional ways that material culture has been studied is to identify ancestral origins, either by actual physical examples or literary and abstract canonical sources. For housing topics this usually entails the formulation of an evolutionary line of development linking early "original" precedent houses to subsequent follower houses. This search-for-original-house-precedent is thus the historic model for upper-class housing research and the basis for assigning ranking and excellence in historic stylistic movements. Unfortunately this connoisseur-like, line-of-elite precedent development is not the way that common houses have been (and still are) created and developed. While popular houses have numerous precedents, both high and low, they do not typically have single, original house precedents in a standard, line-of-influence, creative developmental sense. There simply are no original parent houses for the basic types of common houses analyzed in this book. Therefore, there are no original or first bungalows or first ranches or first four-squares—only previous, gradually evolving bungalows, ranches, and four-squares, developed in vernacular builder progression.[19]

5. Myths about Speculative Building and Builders

There are limited sources and much misinformation about typical common builders and their standard methods of speculative construction. The widespread adoption of speculative building practices in the late nineteenth century solidified the method in which independent small contractors built houses for unknown or "speculative" clients or users. The specific methods and traditions of design, production, and consumption that created these millions of speculative houses have not been well documented and consequently are poorly understood.

This neglect of the building-construction process has produced several major misconceptions about the production of common houses. These include a fundamental misunderstanding of the builder-consumer relationship; inflated assessments of the influence of elite, high-style designs and designers on the production of local builders; the overestimation of the influence of mail-order (Sears), box-car, "kit" houses; and inflated assessments of the number of owner-builders who constructed common houses. While none of these explanations is wrong in itself, each can only be applied to a very small, usually upper-class segment of housing production. They are labeled "misconceptions" here because they do not reflect the method by which the vast majority of America's common houses were actually designed and built by "anonymous" local builders."[20]

6. Myth of the Shrinking Common House

A widely cited interpretation suggests that the size of many popular American houses grew smaller during the early modern period, 1900–1940. Simply stated, this theory hypothesizes that the square footage of most new or remodeled houses was reduced compared to similar houses in previous periods because of the broad impact of technological improvements related to changing patterns of work, domesticity, and gender relations. For the vast majority of working-class Americans, however, those who lived in small, unimproved, two-to-four-room houses and who acquired new improved houses (or expanded existing houses), there was no shrinkage of houses during this period. Rather there were modest increases in size and in standards of living.

This shrinking-house theory was primarily derived from an upper-middle-class literature where the reduction and elimination of servants and the decline in formal patterns of Victorian domesticity were of paramount importance. Yet, even for small numbers of the well-to-do, the data of house size reduction is often misleading or exaggerated because what was actually reduced in size was an upper-class narrative of domesticity. The upper classes continued to inhabit large houses, but the elite status and order of their domestic lives had radically changed. In any case, these upper-class domestic issues had little to do with the previous living conditions of the vast majority of newly ascending working- to middle-class homeowners whose houses did not shrink in comparison to their modest previous dwellings.[21]

This genteel myth of the shrinking house should only be a minor footnote in a book about common houses. Unfortunately, the wide influence of this theory, repeated in the finest scholarship, has resulted in skewed assessments about the making and inhabitation of common housing, especially during the early twentieth century. It is yet another example of how an interpretation borrowed from elite housing trickled down to distort the interpretation of common housing.

7. Myths of Home Ownership and Single-Family Housing

The American dream of home ownership is no myth. Its development has been cited in a vast literature emphasizing its importance as a narrative of ascendancy and improvement for all Americans. Therefore, there is nothing wrong with emphasizing this dominant form of American housing, except that today this story leaves out 40 percent of Americans in multi-unit and rental housing, and, on average historically, more than 50 percent of American families. From the historical perspective of the working to middle class, however, the story is more nuanced and balanced with respect to the ownership of single-family housing. It is a history shaped far more by constraints to ownership than by opportunities and abundance and includes many different types of multi-family rental housing from duplexes to larger rental tenements and apartments. Although not usually included in surveys of housing types, the development of rental and multi-unit houses adds significant comprehensiveness to the story of America's common housing.[22]

8. Myths of Permanence

Common houses are almost always designed and built under economic constraints far more restrictive than upper-class housing. Consequently, their size and amenities are tightly constrained so that they are far more likely to require future modification, remodeling, and expansion (fig. 14). In fact, one might interpret common houses as primarily built with the

Fig. 14. Remodeled and expanded "Polish flats." Raised worker's cottages with multiple additions, Milwaukee, Wisconsin.

intention of inviting and facilitating change to its original fabric and setting. The houses of the upper classes do not typically share these economic limitations and are generally constructed with more permanent materials and in larger sizes that do necessitate substantial additions or replacements (although change may occur for many other reasons). One unfortunate consequence of this permanence and longevity of upper-class houses is that the standard alterations and expansions to common houses have often been perceived negatively, especially by advocates of the historic-preservation movement. By basing standards of historic appreciation or "integrity" largely on the qualities of permanence and unaltered original conditions, the preservation movement has often restricted or eliminated common houses from appreciation and historic designation. Despite widespread recent efforts to include vernacular architecture and environments within the preservation movement, the generally accepted historic criterion of original, unaltered stylistic and construction purity will continue to impose an elite standard that will inhibit the inclusion of common houses in historic review.[23]

Myths and Misconceptions

For readers familiar with the literature of housing, many of these eight "myths" about common dwellings may be surprising and challenging to commonly accepted ideas. In many cases, this problem of interpretation may be resolved once it is realized that, while some ideas may be true for larger, upper-class housing, they may not be true for smaller, much more numerous, middle- to working-class houses. (This problem of housing "class" parallels the discussion of "class" in American society and the shifting boundaries between upper-, middle-, and working-class constituencies about which there is also little agreement.)[24]

Another major reason why ideas about elite, upper-class housing gets mixed up with and misapplied to common housing is because these ideas are assumed to "trickle down" to the builders and residents of common houses. Regrettably, the trickle-down narrative represents a repetitive, long-term cultural problem. Having emphasized this phenomenon, however, it is also important to stress that ideas from an upper class of houses, domesticity, and culture do significantly influence the shape and meaning of common houses—just not so much and not all the time.

2

Underlying Themes for Understanding Common Houses

Floor plans offer an all-purpose cure for many problems of common-house identification and classification. Before presenting floor plans, however, it is important to understand the reasons why plan interpretation is so critical to classification. Three interrelated, underlying themes are most significant: (1) a census method of dominant-type classification, (2) the speculative building methods of local and regional builders, and (3) the importance of local precedents for defining national types. These themes are essential for understanding, not larger middle- to upper-class houses usually classified, but the vast majority of popular, vernacular, everyday, common houses.

A Census Method for Classifying Houses

About the interpretation of vernacular houses, the folklorist Henry Glassie, quoting his mentor Fred Kniffen, has said, "if you can count, you should count."[1] And so we too will count houses, but not just to determine their vast numbers. We need to count common houses in order to establish a census of their dominant types and subtypes in historic progression. When assessing large quantities of common houses, classification by numerical majorities has the potential for producing a readily understandable, comprehensive ranking of dwelling types arranged in historical periods to produce a portrait of popular-housing construction across time (fig. 15).

Without a census method for identifying the most numerically popular forms of housing, common housing research and classification, no matter how well intended, will quickly descend into a quagmire of loosely organized "vernacular types" of seemingly endless variation. (This seems to be the typical status of housing files in state historic-preservation offices where "vernacular" and "non-contributing" designations are frequently employed.) Neighborhood case studies in every part of the country reveal that a census of the most dominant houses, organized primarily by floor-plan type, can form the basis for substantive local, regional, and national

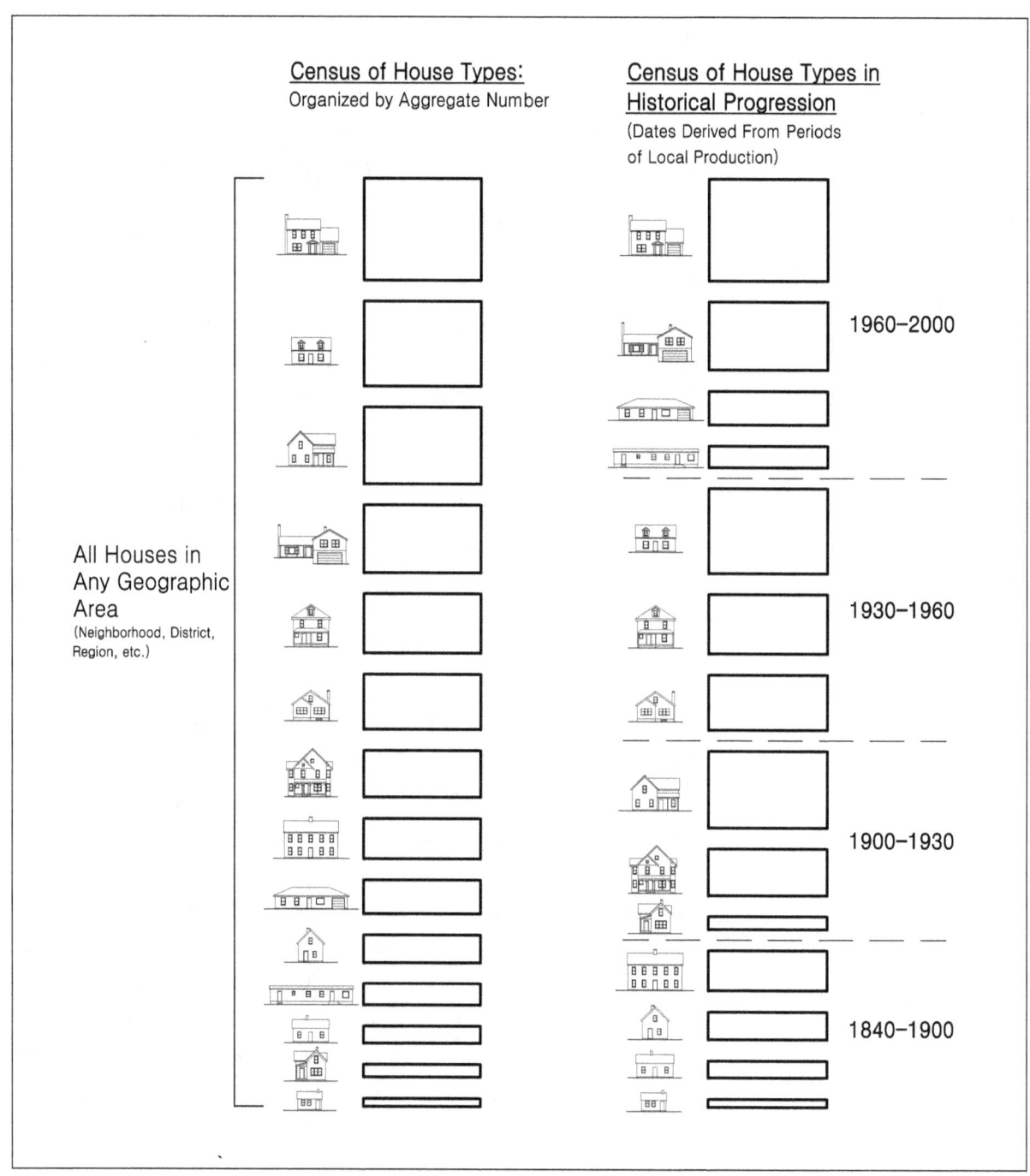

Fig. 15. Census methods for dominant house-type classification. The first column is organized by total aggregate numbers. The second column is organized by the number of houses produced in historical periods.

housing classification. When these majority house types are organized in chronological order, they can help to produce a commonly recognized, demographic portrait of the most popular houses from specific neighborhoods, districts, or regions. In every residential landscape I have observed, I have found that even minimal census estimates of dominant house types (a greatest-hits listing of popular housing in successive periods) will quickly bring clarity to the seemingly impenetrable problems of analysis and classification.[2] (To veterans of housing surveys, this "census method" is another way of describing a reconnaissance survey, with the strategic difference, however, that a numerical census of dominant floor-plan types becomes the primary goal [*IVA*, 23-28]).

A housing census to determine dominant common-house types is an ideal method of classification because common houses were designed, built, and inhabited within constrained economic and cultural contexts where the repetition of well-known houses was, for many different reasons, the standard practice. Unlike the residents and builders of high-style, upper- and upper-middle-class housing, common-house residents did not primarily seek, and common-house builders did not primarily produce, individuality and uniqueness in their housing product, either in their exterior facades or especially in their house plans. Common-house builders, closely attuned to their owners and renters in all periods, have generally reinforced the evolution of proven, familiar housing precedents with only modest degrees of differentiation and individualization between units. These are the similar houses that can readily be quantified in a census of dominant house and plan types and thus form the basis for common housing classification and naming. This does not mean, however, that producing a census of common-house types is simple or easy to obtain—it still requires rigorous investigative fieldwork (including selective interior documentation) and survey experience. But we can be assured that an underlying order, especially of plan type, is almost always present.

This census method stands in contrast to the standard methods of high-style, upper-class housing evaluation and classification. Here individual examples are emphasized without regard to the number of houses actually built. There are no common-house equivalents to such individual masterworks as Mies van der Rohe's Farnsworth House, Frank Lloyd Wright's Fallingwater, and Thomas Jefferson's Monticello. Rather, common houses reach their zenith, not in individual creative difference, but in collective unity with other houses. Usually this collective unity is described negatively as repetition and conformity, but, whatever the ideological interpretation, unified majorities of similar dwellings have defined the standards of appropriateness and popular acceptance in common housing environments. Unlike the creation and marketing of upper-class houses where appreciation is most often awarded to designs of greater individuality and creative uniqueness (and where repetition is a basis for derision and exclusion), the most important "prototype" examples of common houses are actually those that have been built and confirmed in greatest number! Consequently, a census method for counting common houses to determine the most numerous types is not just an efficient means of classification; it is a method that closely reflects the collective values of its builder and consumers in awarding dominant classification to houses confirmed in greatest number (*IVA*, 7–10).

Across the country, in survey areas of varying size within cities, towns, suburbs, and rural areas, I have found that an estimated census of common-house types typically reveals a group of four to eight of the most popular house plans. I call this the "rule of dominant types" because, in hundreds of neighborhoods and survey areas, I have never found a very wide range of the most common house-plan types. Invariably, a majority of local builders, both currently and in previous periods, have narrowed the always wide range of potentially available houses into a more limited range of well-known, frequently repeated, locally accepted types. This rule of dominant house-plan types has occurred with surprising consistency throughout the country and appears to reflect a deep logic of construction and consumption linking local builders and residents in a shared consensus about common housing and domesticity.

It is important to emphasize that the census methods I propose are not new or revolutionary and that various techniques of counting houses, such as reconnaissance surveys, are standard academic and professional procedures. Yet there is a crucial difference. The census method of determining dominant types is not merely a technique of counting and documenting houses but also an evaluative method of classification where the actual numbers of the most common-house types create the criteria or framework for local and regional classification. For many academics and professionals, this is a radical application of census documentation, not just to count houses but to determine the actual basis for assigning housing classification and ranking by aggregate number.

Until quite recently, most survey data gathered by housing professionals and architectural historians were interpreted through elite standards of architectural classification usually emphasizing exterior style and exterior form criteria. Consequently, common houses were seldom evaluated according to their plan types or popular dissemination. Although occasionally informed by actual census estimates, most academic histories and institutional "surveys" of housing have been strongly influenced by other, non-census criteria such as stylistic excellence, original or early period significance, and narratives of upper-class housing development. For example, architectural histories of housing have frequently justified their focus on larger, upper-class houses, in part, by evaluating a region's earliest surviving houses where, predictably, these survivors are often the largest and wealthiest houses.[3] Whether older traditions for avoiding vernacular housing classification in academia and government agencies can be modified and expanded to accommodate the great majority of common housing is an ongoing discussion. The winds of institutional change are certainly in the air, as exhibited by recent National Park Service publications advocating, for example, for greater inclusion of vernacular residential environments in historic documentation.[4] Whatever the influence of these efforts, a census method of dominant house classification holds the greatest promise for accurately interpreting the vast body of difficult-to-classify common housing.

COUNTING HOUSES AND DOMINANT TYPES

Classifying houses according to the diversity of their exterior forms and interior plans and then counting houses to determine which types are the most popular is not a technically complex approach. It is not rocket science, but it does require some explanation. The specific process of assigning meaning and significance to dominant numerical groups is perhaps intuitive, but it also parallels a method borrowed from cognitive science called *prototype theory*. Here we apply this method to determine the dominant types of houses in a "graded notion of categories" based primarily on numbers of houses sharing similar plan types. This strategy differs from standard scientific taxonomy, for example in the biological sciences where the identification of different species, not the counting of individual members of each species, is the primary concern.[5] Here, the counting of the largest numbers of particular house species becomes the dominant criterion for classification. The key census question for common-house classification, therefore, is how to organize and evaluate dominant groups and sub-groups into a meaningful historical interpretive order.

To researchers in the social sciences and city planning as well as to anyone interested in houses, a census of the most popular housing types might seem like a logical approach to the problem of interpreting an astonishingly large number of houses across space and time. For generally speaking, creating categories by counting the number of similar things is a basic method for making sense out of a confusing universe and a basis for scientific classification. Yet, in the vast literature of housing history and typology, the actual counting of houses by form or plan type has seldom been the dominant criterion for interpretation. While smaller, focused, and regional studies often count either specific types of houses or all houses in limited areas, in the majority of works addressing the full range of American housing, interpretive demography has seldom been attempted, although it is often implied in vaguely worded summaries about popular housing. Invariable the best vernacular studies, although limited in scope, are demographically grounded, as in Henry Glassie's *Folk Housing in Middle Virginia,* and Alison K. Hoagland's *Mine Towns: Buildings for Workers in Michigan's Copper Country.*[6]

While census methods may seem logical to general readers, they are not the methods currently used or potentially advocated by academics and housing professionals. There are many reasons both pro and con why census methods might be opposed by professional establishments, which I believe can be summarized as a threat to established professional standards of various types. Perhaps the most neutral thing to be said about census methods is that they will greatly enhance the interpretation and classification of common houses and that such methods need not be applied to already adequately classified, usually upper-class houses (although I believe census evaluation would enhance the evaluation of all housing). In any case, a census method of classification emphasizes one of the most important characteristics of common housing, the general unity of major types, particularly in their floor plans. This underlying unity (based on local variations of national types) is most clearly revealed in the great mountain ranges of American popular housing—ranch, Cape, bungalow, side-hall, four-square, and hall-and-parlor—which will be interpreted in the next chapter.

Local Builders and the Speculative Building Process

The typical ways local and regional builders have constructed common houses tells us a great deal about how these dwellings might be interpreted and classified. Unfortunately, the traditional design and construction methods of common-house builders have not been well recorded. A major source of misinformation has been a failure to interpret the standard way these local builders design and produce houses for unknown clients or users—the speculative building process. Although often perceived negatively, speculative building is the way the overwhelming majority of America's common housing has been constructed since the late nineteenth century. Unless you live in an individually designed or "customized" house or have built your own house, you too probably live in a "spec" house or apartment. That is, a dwelling constructed by a local builder, master builder, contractor, or developer who "speculated" about unknown future residents. Although we do not usually think of our own housing in this commodity production process, most housing has been produced in this manner, especially America's common houses.[7]

Much could be clarified about the speculative building process—for example, how it has changed and evolved historically—but what is important here is the local builders' vernacular method of creating a "local consensus" of house and plan types. Common builders typically develop houses through the influence of many sources, both national and local, professional and vernacular, and high-tech and low-budget. Yet their basic method is to cautiously refine and replicate a familiar repertoire of locally proven prototypes in a design process that can be labeled *composition-decomposition* (fig. 16). It is a vernacular method of coalescing unified designs, most frequently through shared floor plans, to form an informal but highly influential "local consensus" among large numbers of local and regional builders. (This "consensus" does not mean that individual builders actively communicate with each other, only that their acute awareness of each others' work influences local and regional uniformity). It is a method characterized by the refinement of proven prototypes in an evolutionary process far closer to the apprenticeship training in a medieval guild than the pursuit of avant-garde style in an architectural design firm.

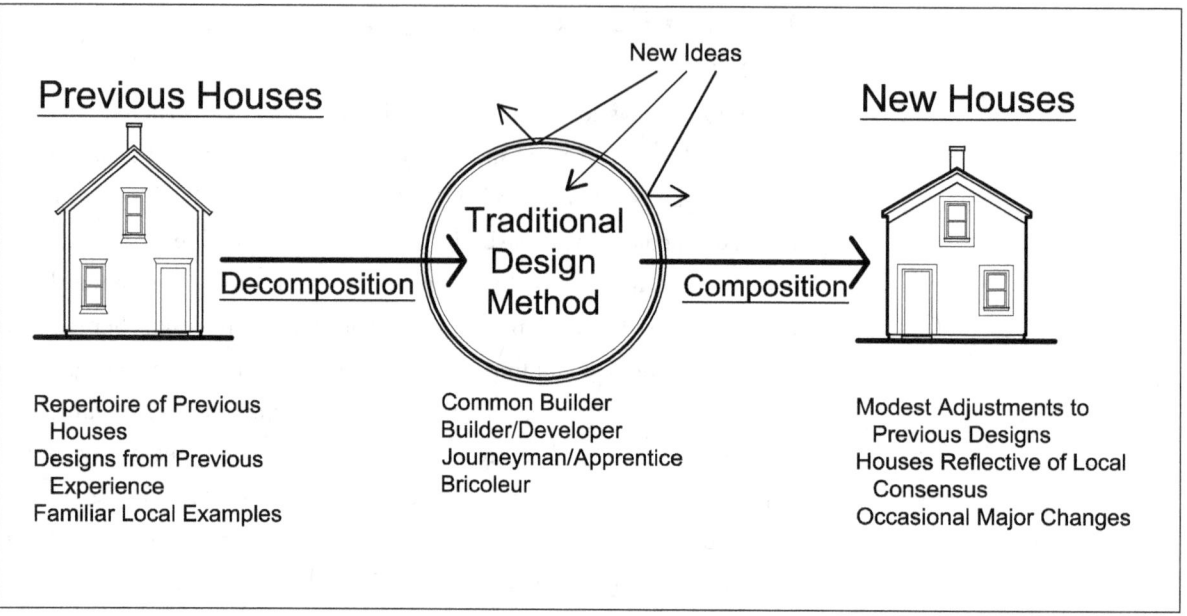

While local builders, past and present, are not unaware of evolving, architect-designed styles in regional and national markets, they chiefly receive their most influential ideas, not top-down, but cautiously sideways, in a builder-to-builder (historically often father-to-son) evolution of proven prototypes and local traditions. Architectural reviewers have criticized this conservative "design method" as unimaginative or just plain copying. Despite a long history of professional criticism, this speculative method has largely produced the underlying unity of America's common houses and floor-plan types.[8] It is the knowledge of these methods that could form the basis for a meaningful classification and nomenclature of common houses.

To summarize the typical way local builders achieve a shared "local consensus" of house types, figure 17 shows four of America's most popular bungalows from around the country. Most literature credits the design "influences" of the bungalow house style to a list of standard sources, including: the European Arts and Crafts movement, Gustav Stickley and *Craftsman* magazine, the works of the architects Greene and Greene and Frank Lloyd Wright, traditional Japanese architecture, English medieval precedents, and various regional architects working in the bungalow style.[9] Often unmentioned, however, is the crucial role of local and regional common-house builders in the translation of these classic sources into the most popular forms of the American bungalow. These popular bungalows, in figure 17, cannot be directly attributed to any of the classic sources without

Fig. 16. Composition-decomposition. Traditional design method of common-house builders. From Thomas Hubka, "Just Folks Designing," *Common Places*.

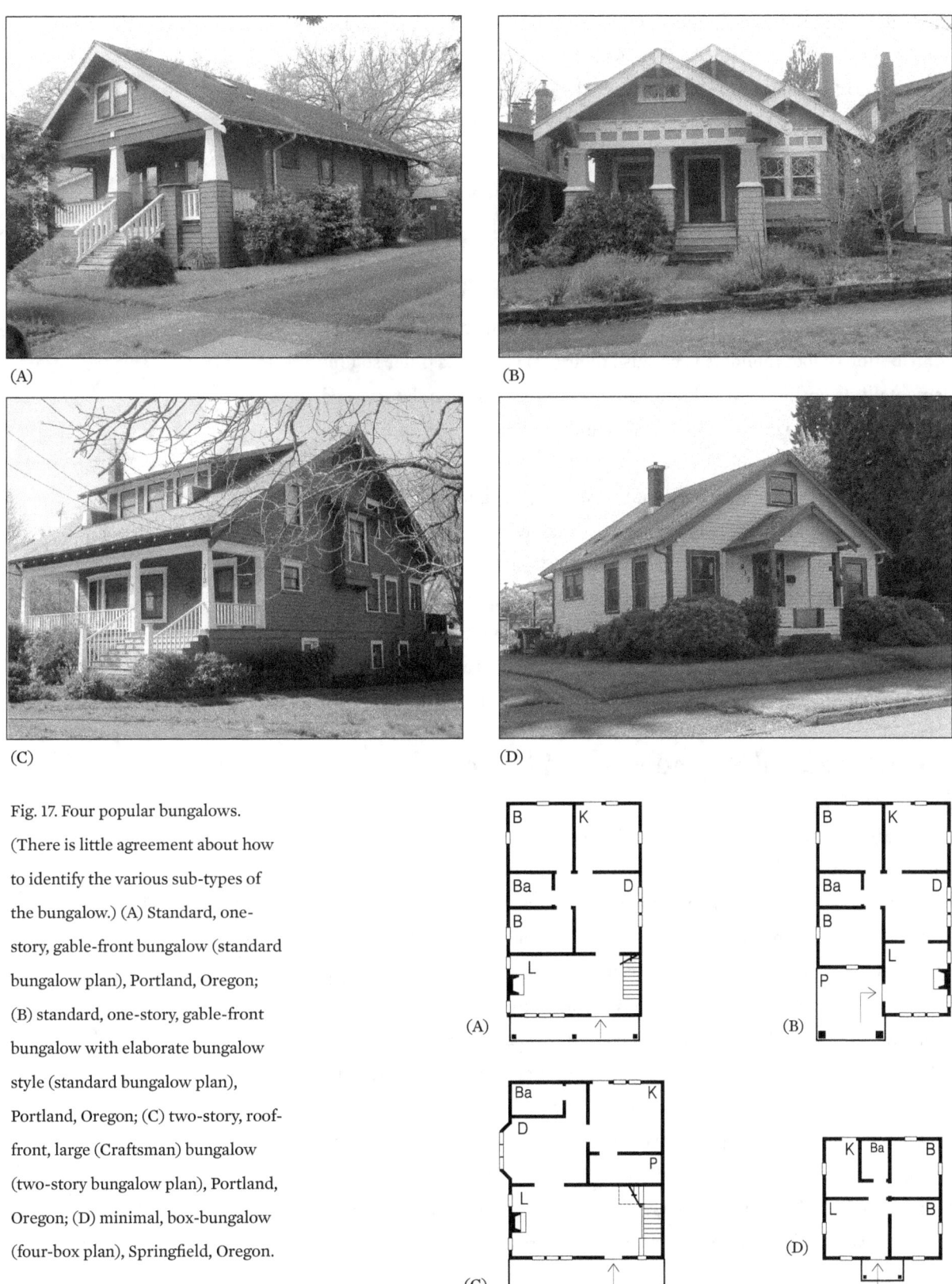

Fig. 17. Four popular bungalows. (There is little agreement about how to identify the various sub-types of the bungalow.) (A) Standard, one-story, gable-front bungalow (standard bungalow plan), Portland, Oregon; (B) standard, one-story, gable-front bungalow with elaborate bungalow style (standard bungalow plan), Portland, Oregon; (C) two-story, roof-front, large (Craftsman) bungalow (two-story bungalow plan), Portland, Oregon; (D) minimal, box-bungalow (four-box plan), Springfield, Oregon.

the critical intermediary catalyst of local builder-designers. In other words, one cannot understand the influence of the standard "sources" on the making of popular bungalows without the transformations performed by hundreds of thousands of "anonymous" local builders. Aided by pattern books and product literature and working in "local consensus," these builders slowly evolved the major types of America's most popular bungalows. This critically important contribution of local builders in this and, indeed, all the dominant types of America's most popular common housing, is seldom acknowledged or analyzed.[10]

One of the main reasons it has been difficult to understand the contribution of local builders is because their basic methods differ so fundamentally from the more widely publicized methods of architects and custom builder-designers of individual houses where creativity, individuality, and uniqueness is most frequently emphasized and evaluated.[11] But in the development of common vernacular houses, the maintenance of tradition and the repetition of slowly evolving successful solutions, adjusted to local conditions, is the standard "design method" (*IVA*, 9-12). While a large middle range of middle- to upper-class housing combines both elite/architect and common/builder design methods, the fundamental differences between these two distinct design traditions are substantial and help to define the basic parameters of the largest portion of common-house development.

Local/Regional Precedents and National Housing Types

Just as the political adage "All politics is local" still rings true, so it is also true that most common houses have strong ties to a local context of building. What is not widely recognized is that building decisions for popular housing are finally interpreted by local builders and contextualized in response to local/regional needs, constraints, and preferences. This insight does not diminish the powerful unifying influences of non-local, national influences in the production of typical common houses, especially as these influences increased throughout the nineteenth century to become truly national house types in the twentieth century. This widely recognized unity of national house types, however, is almost always modified, even today, by regionally distinctive variations. This usually involves the popularization of a limited range of house styles and plan types to create locally dominant vernacular expressions of national types.[12]

Throughout the country, a limited range of locally popularized variants of national house types is the norm. These distinct local types reflect a consensus of local-builder decision-making influenced by local factors such as material distribution, financing, marketing, and land development. In a larger regional comparison, concentrations of single dominant types can be observed in the common houses of Buffalo, Pittsburgh, and Cleveland, neighboring regional cities (fig. 18). Here the dominant forms of each city's most common, late-nineteenth and early twentieth-century housing are surprisingly different where one might expect much more regional and historic unity. While these types of regional differences have narrowed within the last hundred years because of technological and communications standardization, major differences in common-house types still form the basis for local and regional differentiation across the country.[13] To take one specific example, the most popular form of the ranch house in many areas of north Milwaukee has a boxy plan with a detached backyard garage (See figure 18A). Although an unusual ranch in national comparison, this detached-garage ranch is the most dominant form of the ranch in its area. This dominance of the local form of a national type is the norm for common houses throughout America.

Most definitions of American "vernacular" housing are based on pre-1860s, pre-industrial dwellings. These definitions emphasize the importance of indigenous, local expression of place, often as the fundamental basis for establishing local/vernacular identity (*IVA*, 7-8). Yet in an increasingly nationalizing, industrializing housing market after the middle of the nineteenth century, for the largest volume of houses, local/regional vernacular expression gradually gave way to an increasingly unified national housing production system in all but the most isolated, rural areas. Within this larger national context, local/regional building traditions continued to exist, but they were no longer the most dominant influences on the production of popular housing types. Simultaneously, local builders continued to exert regional traditions, not as the dominant determinants of form, but as shapers of locally distinct versions of national types. These keepers of the flame of local building culture, whether small builders or large developers, still play an important role in the translation of national building styles and practices into the local expression of common houses.

Summarizing the collective process by which common builders create a localized consensus of house types, figure 19 shows four locally

dominant ranches. Each example was built many thousands of times to become one of the most numerous types in its particular region. This concentrated uniformity of a few dominant house-plan types out of an always much larger variety of national and regional types is a consistent, fundamental rule of common-house development in all periods and regions.

Another way of understanding the contribution of local houses to the definition of national types is to survey a specific neighborhood or district and identify the local variations of the dominant national types. Almost invariably, such a survey will show that nationally recognized house types have been modified or slightly altered to form local/regional expressions. Figure 20 shows three early twentieth-century houses as constructed in the Buckman neighborhood of Portland, Oregon. Each house reflects a locally interpreted version of a standard house type found throughout the country.

Fig. 18. Popular regional house types. (There are no standard names for these most popular houses.) (A) Two-up, two-down (house plan), Homestead, Pennsylvania; (B) parlor-by-pass plan, Cleveland, Ohio; (C) "telescope" (various side-hall plans), Buffalo, New York.

Fig. 19. Popular regional ranch houses. (There is little agreement about what to call the various subtypes of the ranch.) (A) Narrow-lot ranch (detached-garage plan type), Milwaukee, Wisconsin; (B) standard ranch (standard ranch plan), Portland, Oregon; (C) box-ranch (four-box and garage plan), Springfield, Oregon; (D) garage-in-front ranch (plan), San Fernando Valley, California.

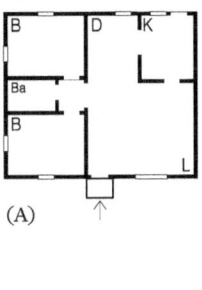
(A)

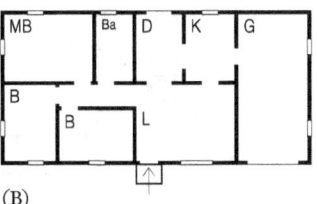
(B)

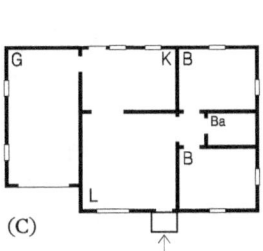
(C)

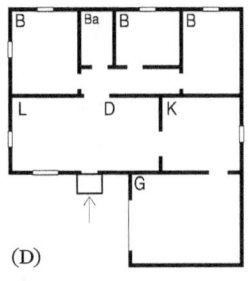
(D)

(A)

(B)

(C)

Fig. 20. Local adaptations of national housing types, Buckman neighborhood, Portland, Oregon: (A) gable-over-porch house form (modified side-hall plan); (B) four-square plan type with standard, extended utility bay addition on the rear; (C) "corner-bay," up-and-down duplex, central-kitchen plan type.

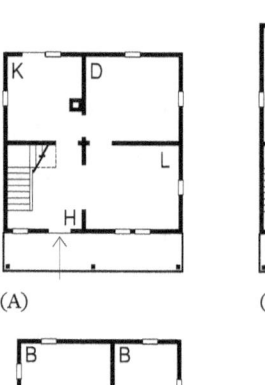
(A)

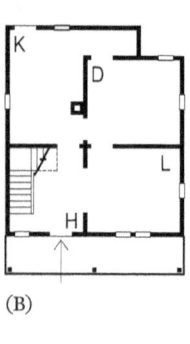
(B)

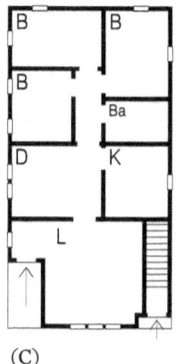
(C)

The source of these local/regional dominant types is the unified, collective actions of local builders selecting and refining a limited range of well-known types. Therefore, when we discuss national building types, such as the ranch, we should really be attempting to grasp the blend of regional ranches (or bungalows or four-squares) that contribute to an always variegated national consensus of popular house types. When we begin to understand this contribution of the local to the national, we will be in a better position to interpret the full range and complexities of common-house development—the combination of dominant local prototypes (for example, all the ranches in figure 19) into a variegated, national consensus of dominant national housing types.

It is sometimes challenging to distinguish between the local/regional, facts-on-the-ground expression of common houses and the larger national/regional expressions of similar houses. While I have emphasized the often overlooked frequency of local housing differentiation, it is equally important to recognize the broad national unity among many types of common houses, sometimes defying regional differentiation. For the last 150 years, America's most common houses have increasingly shared fundamental similarities reflecting the influence of unifying, increasingly national systems of mass communications, housing literature, marketing techniques, housing technologies, financing, design, manufacturing, and site/land development. Consequently, America's largest groups of common houses—from workers' cottages and four-squares in the nineteenth century to bungalows, Capes, and ranch houses in the twentieth century—clearly demonstrate strong similarities and basic patterns of house and plan standardization.[14] Despite this consistency, however, particular characteristics are almost always present in the local expression of these national types. Furthermore it is the consistent dominance of a few locally selected houses from a much larger repertoire of national house types that today most often gives unique character to the local housing landscape. Therefore, it is not the widely recognized influence of the national on the local but the unpredictable, variegated, and poorly understood influence of the local on the national that now requires our concentrated attention.

3

EMPHASIZING THE FLOOR PLAN IN COMMON HOUSES

From the outside, the three Milwaukee houses in figure 21 share many features. They have similar facades, they are extremely difficult to classify by architectural style, they have no commonly accepted names, even locally, and they exist in great numbers both in Milwaukee and, in similar forms, throughout America. Yet, behind their facades, these three houses are fundamentally different from each other in relation to their floor plans and domestic usage. They are, in fact, three of Milwaukee's most popular houses, which no assessment of the city's domestic architecture should confuse.[1] Alternatively, the three Portland, Oregon, houses in figure 22 appear strikingly different and demonstrate a typical range of pre–World War II "period revival" and "minimal traditional" exterior styles. Yet these three houses are fundamentally similar on the inside and share floor plans with similar pattern of domestic usage, despite their exterior diversity.[2]

Both sets of houses illustrate different aspects of a basic problem that has plagued common-house interpretation—facade/plan interchangeability. This problem emerged during the second half of the nineteenth century in a period of rapid industrialization when the traditional relationship between house facade and floor plan became uncoupled. Consequently both facades and plans became interchangeable components in what might ironically be interpreted as a type of modern, interchangeable-part design relationship (fig. 23). After more than a century, this practice of facade/plan interchangeability has become a nearly universal characteristic of popular housing in the United States and throughout the industrialized world.[3] The inability to resolve (or even identify) this fundamental issue of housing nomenclature is demonstrated by the Milwaukee examples with the same style on the outside and different plans on the inside (see fig. 21), and by the Portland examples with different styles on the outside and the same plan on the inside (see fig. 22).

Fig. 21. Three Milwaukee, Wisconsin, houses. Similar exterior facades, different interior plans and domestic functions. (A) Parlor-by-pass entry cottage (parlor-by-pass plan); (B) standard bungalow (plan); (C) Polish flat, raised worker's cottage plan, converted to duplex.

This mutual flexibility of outside facades to inside plans has posed consistent problems of interpretation for all systems of architectural housing classification and nomenclature, as confirmed in each of the twenty-six metropolitan regions investigated for this study. Since the late nineteenth century, however, architectural theorists, architects, and particularly modernists have condemned facade and plan interchangeability as a sham, dishonest practice of common builders. Consequently, this method has been condemned in literature both high and low, and, not surprisingly, few housing classification systems have adequately interpreted (or even addressed except to criticize) this fundamental characteristic of domestic construction. Despite this criticism, facade/plan interchangeability has remained a continuous practice for over 150 years to become the accepted norm for most housing construction in America except for the most expensive and individualistic dwellings. It is time to attempt a more neutral

EMPHASIZING THE FLOOR PLAN | 49

(A)

(B)

(C)

(A, B, C)

Fig. 22. Three Portland, Oregon, houses. Different exterior facades, similar interior plans and domestic functions. (There is little agreement about what to call these houses.)
(A) Minimal-traditional style (expanded four-box plan);
(B) minimal-traditional, modern Cape style (expanded four-box plan);
(C) period revival, Tudor/English (style expanded four-box plan).

evaluation of facade/plan interchangeability and to adjust current systems of classification to this ubiquitous practice.

In order to address these and many other fundamental deficiencies of common-house interpretation, the principle of a two-part identification formula is recommended—a combination of outside and inside labeling. Typically this couplet would link a term interpreting exterior style or form with a term interpreting floor plan or room usage. (For example, a Federal-style, center-chimney plan, house; a Craftsman bungalow, four-box plan, house.) For those familiar with common-house nomenclature, even this simple formula might seem too complex because some houses can simply be identified with one term—for example, the four-square, three-decker, and split-level. It is important to recognize, however, that such single-word/phrase houses are the exceptions, not the rule. Furthermore, in houses with successful single-term labels, many distinct interior and exterior characteristics are encapsulated within the single term. Therefore, through common usage, the widely recognized four-square house, named for the interior plan of its four ground-floor rooms, is also recognized for its distinctive cubic two-story exterior form, often with a long porch and a low hip-roof. This kind of inside/outside recognition is what successful nomenclature can accomplish. Unfortunately, the vast majority of America's common houses cannot be identified by simple, one-term labels. Because exterior terms are better established, the addition of a term to describe the interior floor plan would bring substantial clarity to common-house interpretation. This emphasis on plan is not meant to supplant or de-emphasize existing exterior classification, which is always essential for identification. We just need to supply some more information about a common house than its typical facade and shape can offer. And a floor plan is a good place to start.

Classifying by Floor-Plan Type

Classification by floor plan has many distinct advantages for the interpretation of common houses. These include: (1) Distinct floor-plan types—a clear differentiation exists between basic plans throughout the nation permitting highly uniform classification. (2) Universality of the floor plan—every house has a floor plan, and no house is unqualified or excluded, as in stylistic classification. (3) Accessibility and user-friendliness—a familiarity with floor plans and how they function underlies the way most people understand, talk about, and select housing. Unlike the obscure language of architectural style, basic floor-plan relationships, like the number of bedrooms and baths, familiar to most users, provide a solid foundation for common-house interpretation. And (4), plans from exterior observation—basic floor-plan information can usually be obtained from exterior analysis because of the basic similarity of common-house plan types throughout America.

Of these advantages, the first, the existence of distinct floor-plan types, is the most important criterion for identifying common houses. Concealed behind minimally detailed, often similar-looking, exterior facades are distinctly different types of floor plans that have a high degree of regional uniformity and are usually identifiable from exterior observation. Typically this diversity takes the form of a small number of well-known, dominant types in local/regional consensus. As might be expected, there are hundreds of different plan types and subtypes within the estimated

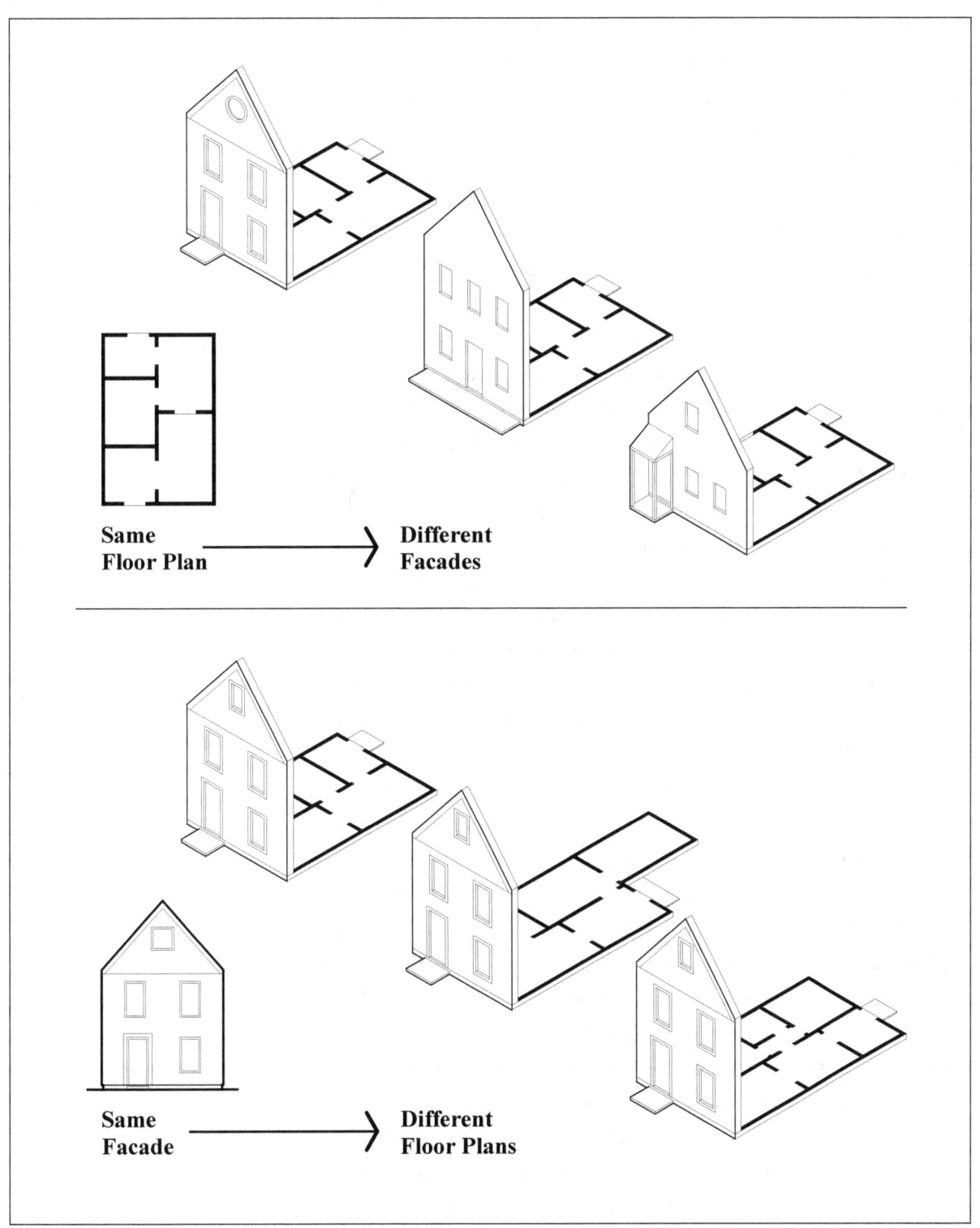

Fig. 23. Interchangeability of exterior facades and interior floor plans.

80 million current houses constructed for over two hundred years in the United States. Yet, despite these overwhelming numbers, there is a surprising consistency in the typical local/regional range of basic house and floor-plan types, providing a critically important starting point for interpreting and classifying common houses.

Plan Prototypes

Since there is no current or historic census of common-house plans, a group of estimated generic, prototype plans is presented as a preliminary typological framework. Figure 24 shows fourteen of the most common single-family, prototype floor plans culled from the housing literature, extensive interviews with local and regional authorities, and over ten years of case-study fieldwork in twenty-six metropolitan and rural areas from throughout the country.[4] These most common prototypes are arranged in four historic periods based on estimates of the most commonly constructed house plans from throughout the country.

These prototype plans were drawn as diagrams representing typical, generic room organizations characteristic of a range of similar floor plans. Each diagram shows the location of three of the most important rooms—kitchen, living room, and bedrooms—and including other critical components of the domestic plan: entrances, stairs, fireplace/stoves, bathrooms, and subordinate rooms.

Each prototype plan was selected to represent a larger family of related house plans united by multiple developmental sources, including early settlement patterns, ethnic traditions, material and construction techniques, and various regional developments. While there are several widely published typologies of pre-modern house-plan types (for example, English traditions of American Colonial houses), these earlier traditions were generally diffused in complex stages of national industrialized development beginning in the second half of the nineteenth century. Consequently, when assessing the massive volume of currently existing common houses, it is important to recognize multiple, simultaneous lines of development with multiple overlapping sources, as demonstrated in the multi-sourced development of the popular bungalow and ranch.[5] Likewise, the names for each prototype house plan are at best a compromise between many competing interpretations and regional variations and are indicative of the typical Tower of Babel dilemmas for classifying and naming common houses.

EMPHASIZING THE FLOOR PLAN | 53

Plan Prototypes & House Plans, 1800-2000

I. Pre-Modern Prototypes (1800 - 1860):

1) One-Room Plan Types

aka: (No standard names)
One-Room House
Early Settlement House
Cabin
Single-Cell
Dates: Pre 1800-1860+
Plan: 1 room deep
1 room wide
Stories: 1, 1½
Rooms: 1, 1½ (total)

House/Plan Types

One-Room (Side Entry) | One-Room (Short-End Entry)

Summary: All immigrant and indigenous groups had one-room house plans although the English "hall" dominates the early American development. In all regions, early settlement, one-room log, frame, or temporary structures often preceded later dwellings and were frequently incorporated within later structures. Although romanticized in pioneer accounts, under-recorded, one-room houses were continuously built in all regions for modest and marginal houses into the 20th century. (One-room houses have often been interpreted as a sub-set of one-room-deep houses, below.)

2) Two-Room & One-Room-Deep Plan Types

aka: Hall-and-Parlor
"I"-House
Center Passage
Single-Pile
Dates: Pre 1800-1900
Plan: 1 room deep
2-2½ rooms wide
Stories: 1, 1½, 2
Rooms: 2-3 (1st fl.)
2-6 (total)

House/Plan Types

Center Passage | Center Chimney | Hall Entry | Rowhouse Type

Summary: The English tradition of two-room, single-family, side entry, one-room-deep houses in one-and two-story forms dominates the early American development. The major plan types differ in their entranceways, either entering directly into the hall or living room from the outside or into a central entrance hall or passageway. By 1820, rear additions, containing a relocated kitchen, became standard so that later versions were typically built with an attached kitchen in a T-or L-shaped plan. There are many variations in the location of fireplaces/stoves and stairs. The gable-entry "two-over-two" version of this plan (one of Pittsburgh and Cincinnati's most popular houses) is more directly related to the English side-hall, row-house plan but is included here as a variation of a two-room-on-the-first-floor plan. The southern shotgun house plan, a unique type of one-room wide houses, from African/Creole/French traditions could be included here but it is unrelated to the dominant traditions of English, one-room-deep houses.

Fig. 24. (pages 53–61) Plan prototypes and house plans. Fourteen of America's most popular plan prototypes with related house plans, 1800–2000.

With a few exceptions, most common American house plans can be organized within the fourteen prototypes in figure 24. Considering the complexity of the topic and the lack of basic surveys, these prototype plans must be considered a very preliminary, estimated summary of basic generic types for which there could just as easily be thirteen, fifteen, or twenty-seven prototype plans. Hopefully this template will serve as a preliminary proposal for improving the classification of America's most popular single-family house-plan types.

Plan Prototypes & House Plans, 1800-2000

I. Pre-Modern Prototypes (1800 - 1860):

3) Two-Room-Deep Plan Types

aka: Central Passage Plan
Georgian Plan
Two Room Deep Plans
Double Pile
Dates: Pre 1800-1860
Plan: 2 rooms deep
2½ rooms wide
Stories: 1½, 2, 2½
Rooms: 5 (1st fl.)
9-10 (total)

House/Plan Types

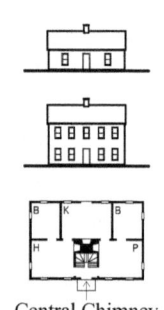
Central Passage

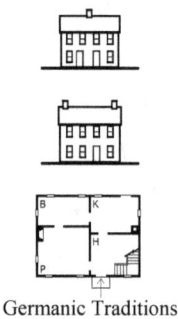
Central Chimney

Germanic Traditions

Summary: English and German traditions dominate the early American development of two-room deep houses. English plans are usually symmetrical with central entrance halls and German plans are often asymmetrical with and without entrance halls. Both traditions locate the stairway at, or near the center of the plan. By the second half of the 19th century, both traditions evolved into many hybrid variations in increasingly national plan types that have continued to be constructed into the 21st century. In most periods and regions, two-story, two-room-deep houses were middle to upper-class dwellings but there are many modest variations of this basic plan type. The Cape Cod plan is a 1-1/2 story version of the standard English, two-story, two-room-deep plan. The related "saltbox plan" is a transitional house type inbetween one-and two-rooms-deep traditions.

4) Side-Hall Plan Types

aka: (No standard plan names)
Side-Hall Plan
Rowhouse Plan
Half-House Plan
Dates: Pre 1800-1900
Plan: 2-3 rooms deep
1½ rooms wide
Stories: 1, 1½
Rooms: 3-4 (1st fl.)
4-8 (total)

House/Plan Types

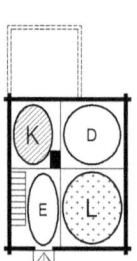

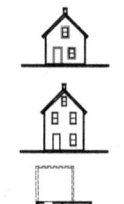
Side-Hall

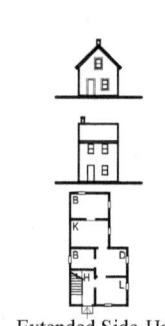
Extended Side-Hall

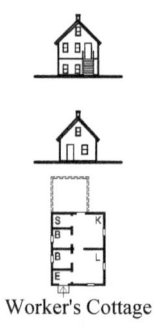
Worker's Cottage

Summary: The side-hall plan, with the stair hallway to one side of the front facade, existed in most European urban cultures that settled America although English versions derived from two-story, attached row-houses were most influential. In America, the side-hall plan also became a free-standing house, and in many variations, it is one of the most popular and continuously built house plans in the 19th and early 20th centuries. The consistent plan organization locates the stairway in a one-half-room wide stair hall placed to one side of the front facade. Houses with side-hall plans were most often built with extended back "ells" or additions that became permanent features in various regional developments. A one-story, worker's cottage plan is included as a distantly related one-and one-half room wide plan organization but without a second floor and stairway.

Plan Prototypes & House Plans, 1800-2000

II. Transitional Prototypes (1820 - 1900):

5) Side-Gable Plan Types

aka: Cross-wing/Side-Gable
Temple-and-Wing
Upright-and-Wing
T-Plan
Dates: 1800-1900
Plan: 1-2 rooms deep
2-3 rooms wide
Stories: 1, 1½, 2
Rooms: 3-5 (1st fl.)
4-10 (total)

House/Plan Types

Side-Gable | Expanded Side-Gable

Summary: The cross-wing house has a distinctive T-shaped plan with the kitchen usually located in the side gable although some plans place the kitchen at the rear of the front gable. Despite its widespread popularity, there is no regional or even local agreement about what to call this house type. Unusual for common housing, the kitchen was most often placed on the front side of the house. This kitchen in the side-gable was built in one-and two-story forms with the side gable either one- or two-rooms deep. Variations of the plan have two front doors entering the front parlor and the kitchen. The popular development of this plan followed early 19th century western expansion to become a dominant Midwest farmhouse type. The cross-wing is one of the most popular pre-1900 farm house plans throughout America as for example in New York, Wisconsin, and Oregon.

6) Parlor By-Pass Plan Types

aka: (No standard plan names)
Parlor By-Pass Plan
Side Porch Plan
Dates: 1880-1910
Plan: 3 rooms deep
1-2 rooms wide
Stories: 1, 1½, 2
Rooms: 3-4 (1st fl.)
4-6 (total)

House/Plan Types

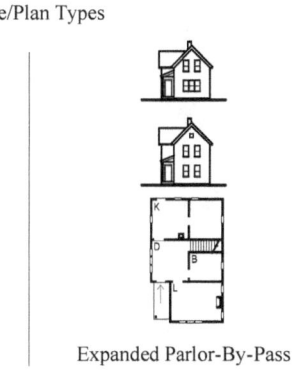

Parlor-By-Pass | Expanded Parlor-By-Pass

Summary: In a unique entry sequence, the front room or parlor nearest the street was "by-passed" by an entrance porch leading to the second room, usually a type of entry-dining room. Nationally, elaborate forms of this plan were built in the Queen Anne style and the house is sometimes called a Queen Anne or Victorian cottage. The basic plan was built, however, in simpler styles as for example in the Cleveland area where it was one of the most popular pre-1930 houses. In various one-and two-story forms it was built in both working-and middle-class neighborhoods.

Plan Prototypes & House Plans, 1800-2000

II. Transitional Prototypes (1820 - 1900):

7) Victorian House/Expanded Side-Hall Plan Types

aka: Victorian Cottage/House
Queen Anne Cottage/House
English Traditional
Dates: 1850-1920
Plan: 3 rooms deep
2 rooms wide
Stories: 1½, 2, 2½
Rooms: 5-8 (1st fl.)
7-16 (total)

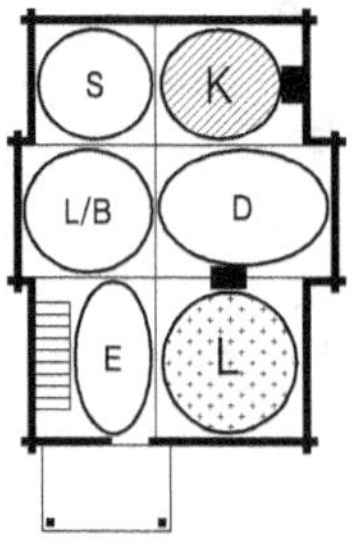

House/Plan Types

Victorian House  | Expanded Side-Hall

Summary: There is no common name for this basic Victorian era middle to upper-class house plan. It is an enlarged version of the side-hall plan, two full rooms wide, three rooms deep, and a full second floor. It was often one of the first house plans to contain electricity, gas, and a full bath on the second floor. It was most numerously built nationally in modest, boxy, four-room, ground floor plans (which is why it is included in this list of "common houses"), but it is best known in larger, elaborate "Queen Anne" versions with room projections, elaborate bays, dormers, and turrets to become a standard upper- class Victorian house. In larger versions, the plan is organized in many different types of customized double parlor plan organizations.

Plan Prototypes & House Plans, 1800-2000

III. Early Modern Prototypes (1890 - 1950):

8) Four-Square Plan Types

aka: Four Square
Midwest Cube
Four Box
Dates: 1860-1920
Plan: 2 rooms deep
2 rooms wide
Stories: 1, 1½, 2, 2½
Rooms: 4-5 (1st fl.)
4-9 (total)

House/Plan Types

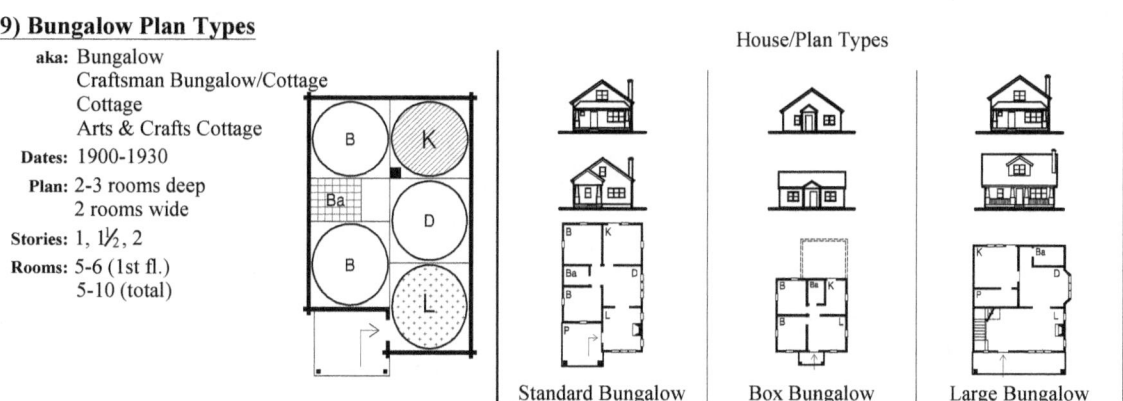

Four-Square   Four Box

Summary: The four-square plan is one of the most uniform and well-known pre-WWII floor plans in America. In its most popular form with a low hip-roof and hip-roof dormer, it defies a stylistic label; hence its unique name derived from its plan. (Common houses are seldom named or primarily understood for their floor plans.) The four-square is one of the first, popular middle-class houses with electricity and a three-fixture, second floor bath. Earlier versions have an entrance room with a prominent stairway while later versions locate a less visible double-back stair between the entrance hall and the kitchen. A distantly related version of this plan is the modest one-story, four-box which shares the four-quadrant division of the plan without a stair-hall or a second floor.

9) Bungalow Plan Types

aka: Bungalow
Craftsman Bungalow/Cottage
Cottage
Arts & Crafts Cottage
Dates: 1900-1930
Plan: 2-3 rooms deep
2 rooms wide
Stories: 1, 1½, 2
Rooms: 5-6 (1st fl.)
5-10 (total)

House/Plan Types

Standard Bungalow   Box Bungalow   Large Bungalow

Summary: The bungalow in its many versions is probably America's most popular pre-1930 house plan. The term bungalow creates confusion not only because of its exotic Asian origins but because it is a name for both the architectural style and a type of floor plan. The standard one-story, five-to-six room plan arrangement aligns a living-dining-kitchen along one side and bedrooms and bath along the other. This one-story plan is found in single-family, duplex and multi-unit houses. It was the first modern house with electricity and a three-fixture bath for an expanding working-to middle-class. The basic amenities of the bungalow plan could be minimized in a four-room, box-bungalow plan and expanded in larger Arts and Craft or Craftsman versions with second floor master bedrooms and baths. For working-to middle-class families, it was the first exposure to a type of open plan with a living room and dining room open to each other.

Plan Prototypes & House Plans, 1800-2000

III. Early Modern Prototypes (1890 - 1950):

10) Period Revival & Minimal Traditional Plan Types

aka: (No standard plan names)
Period Revival Plan
Minimal-Traditional Plan
Storybook/Cottage Plan
Tudor Cottage

Dates: 1920-1980

Plan: 2-2½ rooms deep
2-2½ rooms wide

Stories: 1, 1½, 2

Rooms: 4-6 (1st fl.)
5-9 (total)

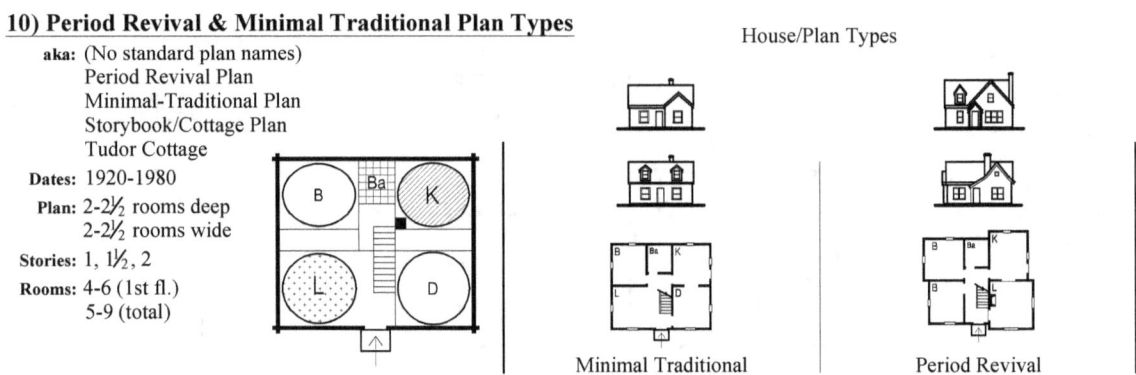

Summary: Period revival and minimal traditional house plans were developed in the 1920s and surpassed the bungalow plan by 1930. Although exterior styles alternated between European romantic (period revival) and Colonial Revival (Cape Cod) styles, their floor plans were built in a standardized (but as yet unnamed) 1-1/2 story, expanded-room-at-each-corner floor plan with a master bedroom and bath on the first floor. This house type is more widely recognized in larger "period revival" styled houses with more complex individualized plans and larger second floors. There is no agreed upon name for this house type in smaller, much more regular versions with unified plans. Larger period revival plans contain a master bedroom and bath on the second floor while standard, minimal traditional versions locate the master bedroom and bath on the first floor. Versions of this difficult to label, ubiquitous floor plan continued to be built after WWII, for example in Levittown developments and into the second half of the 20th century.

Plan Prototypes & House Plans, 1800-2000

IV. Modern Prototypes (1940 - 2000):

11) Ranch Plan Types

aka: Ranch
Suburban Ranch
American Ranch
Dates: 1940-1990
Plan: 2 rooms deep
3-5 rooms wide
Stories: 1
Rooms: 5-10 (total)

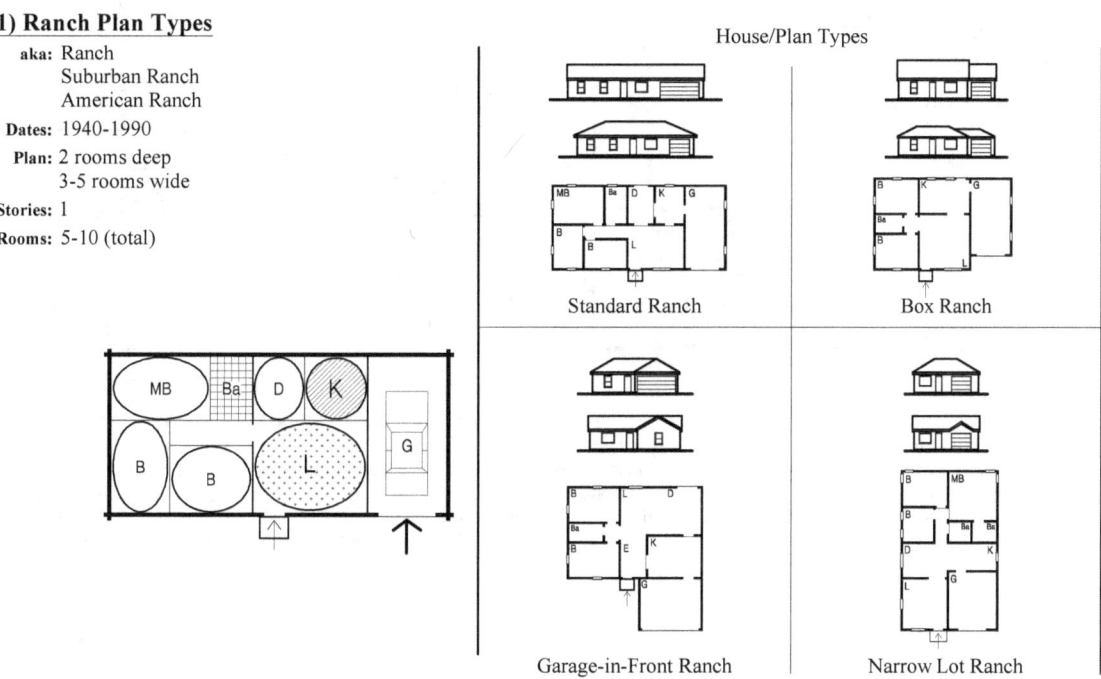

Summary: The ranch house in its many versions is America's most popular plan type. It is the dominant single-family post-WWII, suburban house in most regions and metropolitan areas throughout the country. The one-story ranch house floor plan radically reoriented the American home which had consistently privileged the two-story house as a cultural ideal. It was the first popular house to fully integrate the garage into the house plan. In its most popular arrangement, the plan is divided into three zones: garage, living, and sleeping areas. The different types of ranch houses primarily differ in their garage placement, the orientation of the length and width of the basic rectangular shape to the street, and the number of bedrooms, baths, and garages. Although the major construction era is 1950-1980, ranch house plans continued to be built into late 20th century.

Plan Prototypes & House Plans, 1800-2000

IV. Modern Prototypes (1940 - 2000):

12) Split-Level Plan Types

aka: Split-Level Ranch
Up & Down Plan
Split-Entry Plan

Dates: 1960-1990

Plan: 2 rooms deep
3-4 rooms wide

Stories: 2

Rooms: 3-8 (1st fl. & Garage)
7-10 (total)

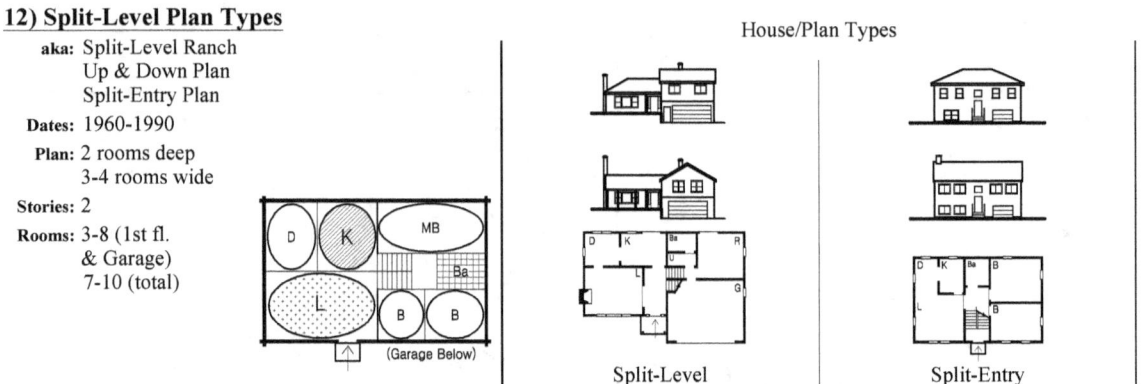

House/Plan Types

Split-Level | Split-Entry

Summary: The construction of split level and split entry houses parallels ranch plan development. The split-level plan responds to narrower lots and accomodates grade-level changes better than the ranch plan. The split-level floor plan is divided into the same three-part zones as the ranch except the zones are located on three separated floors linked by half-floor stairs. Typically the living area is located to one side on the middle, ground level, with the bedroom area located above the garage to the other side. The split-entry house plan is related to the split-level house because of its split-level front entrance stairway, but it is actually a basic two story suburban house with an unusual split-level, entrance stairway.

Plan Prototypes & House Plans, 1800-2000

IV. Modern Prototypes (1940 - 2000):

13) Suburban Minimal-Traditional Plan Types

aka: (No Standard Names)
Suburban Housing
Developer Housing
Colonial Revival
McMansion
Dates: 1950-2000
Plan: 2-3 rooms deep
2-5 rooms wide
Stories: 1½, 2, 2½
Rooms: 3-10 (1st fl.)
6-16 (total)

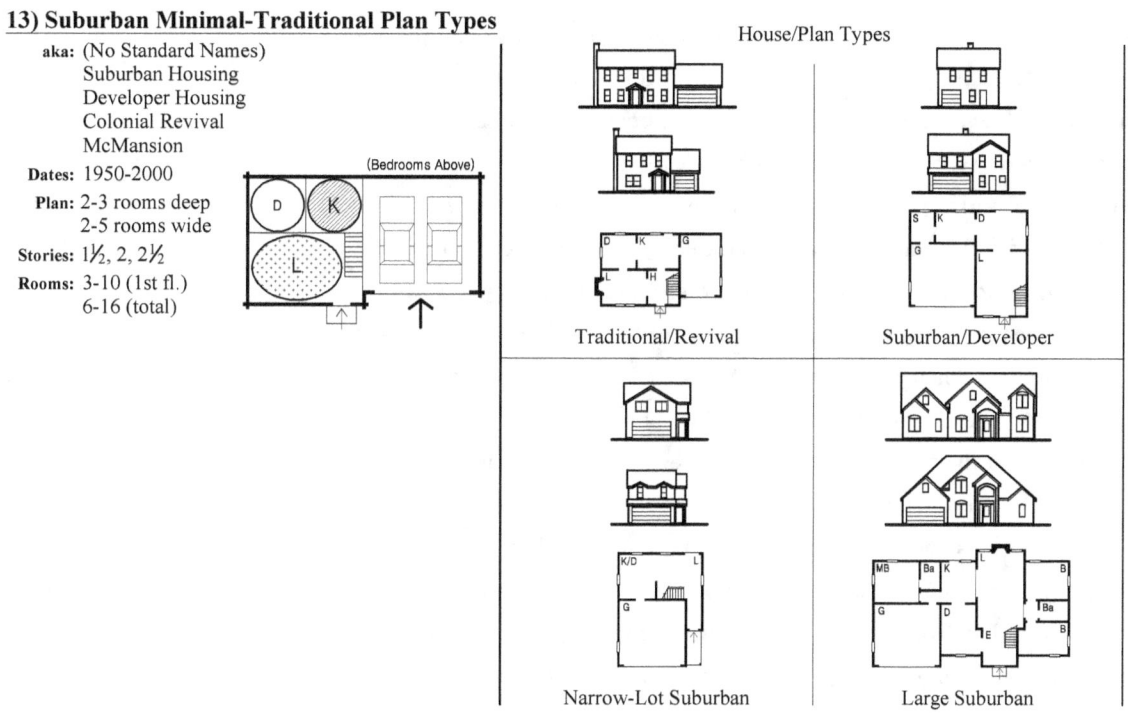

Traditional/Revival · Suburban/Developer · Narrow-Lot Suburban · Large Suburban

Summary: There is little agreement about identification and classification of the most popular, two-story, single-family suburban housing of the last quarter of the 20th century. Throughout the country ubiquitous, two-story houses with integrated garages were built in a variety of floor plan types. Most houses combine minimal traditional, vaguely Colonial styled exteriors with two-room-deep plans, living areas and kitchens on the first floor, and sleeping areas on the second. In larger versions with multi-gables they have been labeled McMansions and display more European architectural detailing for middle-to-upper class residents.

14) Manufactured Home Plan Types

aka: Trailer
Mobile Home
Double-wide
Dates: 1930-2000
Plan: 1-2 rooms deep
5-6 rooms wide
Stories: 1
Rooms: 4-10 (total)

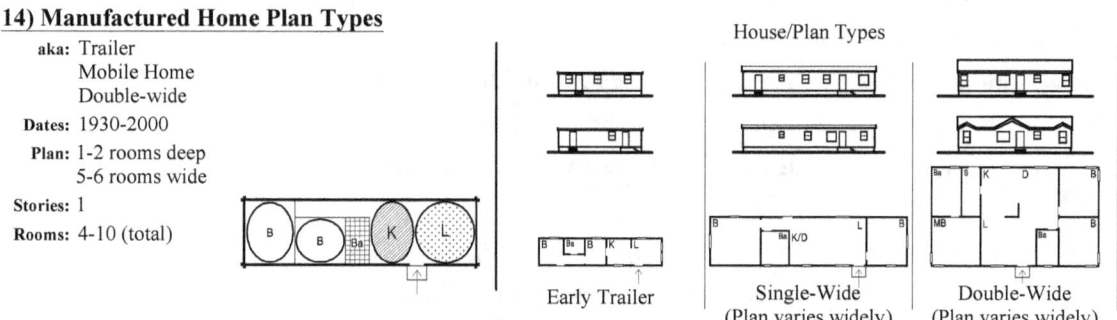

Early Trailer · Single-Wide (Plan varies widely) · Double-Wide (Plan varies widely)

Summary: First called trailers because of their wheels and mobility, manufactured homes have maintained 5-10% of the American housing market for half a century. Restricted in width by highway transportation requirements, the standard unit has been upgraded with modern technological and domestic comfort features but the basic plan has remained consistent with kitchen/dining/living at one end and bedrooms at the opposite end. The major change in plan type has been the development of double-wide units, combining two units side-by-side to create many new types of house plans.

Dominant House Plans, c. 1800–2000

To the right of each of the fourteen prototype diagrams in figure 24 are what might cautiously be labeled America's most popular common-house plans. It is a preliminary estimate of thirty-eight of the most numerous single-family house plans in successive historical periods during the last two hundred years. These thirty-eight plans, however, must still be considered generic types because, as we have stressed, regional variations of national house-plan types can be found throughout the country. In fact, local and regional variations of these national types guarantee that this list is not entirely accurate for any particular district or region of the country.

The thirty-eight dominant house-plan types in figure 24 are based on estimated national censuses of the most dominant numerical house plans in historic sequence. Since there are no national house-type surveys, even for currently existing houses, these census estimates are primarily based on a very limited range of case-study surveys from throughout the country as well as housing estimates from regional scholars and a limited literature. Other potential shortcomings of this list include: (A) An absence of multi-unit house types. Examples of multi-unit housing, from the ubiquitous duplex to larger multi-unit apartment buildings, could not be included because of their complexity in comparison to single-family plans. (B) An absence of major regional houses. Significant examples of local and regional houses, like the raised worker's cottage of the upper Midwest and the shotgun's distinct camelback, are not included, because they become less numerous in a national survey. (C) An absence of extensive subtypes. For readers of more focused housing surveys, such as Herbert Gottfried and Jan Jennings's *American Vernacular Buildings and Interiors* and Daniel D. Reiff's *Houses from Books*, there is an absence of many housing subtypes, particularly from the late nineteenth century. These could not be included in such a broad national survey.

Despite these limitations, the prototype plans in figure 24 are intended to promote an assessment of the vast contours of regional and national housing development. I hope the chart inspires future studies to be guided by census-informed surveys, which are critical components to bringing greater clarity and accuracy to the interpretation of common housing. Whatever their limitations, these prototype plans also offer an alternative summary comparison to the standard histories of American housing as compiled by architectural historians, architects, and geographers.

Figure 24 clearly demonstrates fundamental differences in housing selection between this census-estimated survey and the standard histories of American housing. Most of these histories, while often implying a demographic basis for housing selection, are typically summaries of upper- and upper-middle-class housing development. Usually these surveys are organized according to a chronology of stylistic development emphasizing examples of unique masterworks, both elite and vernacular. When common houses are included, their examples are quite selective and are usually drawn from either early settlement periods, when the housing of all classes was more uniform, or they reflect elite interpretations of housing history based primarily on stylistic development.[6] Figure 24, however, is a proposal for what a history of American housing might look like if the goal were to portray the popular development of housing.

Classifying Houses by Room Function and Usage

I have classified house plans according to the arrangement or organization of their rooms. While individual room function is usually assumed, the spatial arrangement of rooms, not usage, has guided my standard analysis. Yet common houses can also be analyzed according to their domestic function, and there are many distinct advantages for doing so.

Functional analysis may begin simply by recording the room name and usage: living, dining, kitchen, bedroom, etc. Thus labeling room usage can be a first step toward interpreting the historic rhythms of domestic life that structure and are structured by the way houses function for their inhabitants. Labeling room function is a basic way most people talk about and evaluate houses. While under-emphasized in architectural history, the interpretation of room usage in floor plans has the potential to transform and humanize the study of common housings by shifting the focus of analysis from the spatial container to the usage of rooms by their inhabitants.

As a method of spatial analysis, the floor plan has enjoyed almost universal usage in most cultures. Floor plans have been used so regularly probably because they summarize such a broad range of important information about a house, but principally they can provide a spatial analysis of the way a house is used. The classic summary of the logic of the floor plan, "form follows function," unites the spatial "form" or plan organization of rooms with the domestic "function" or usage of the rooms.[7]

Floor Plans and Domestic Function, c. 1800–2000

The literature of housing offers many ways to interpret the domestic function or usage of house and home.[8] There are three basic patterns of room usage and domestic function that underlie the historic development of domestic space and domesticity within common American houses: 1) kitchen-centered to multi-centered living (fig. 25); 2) increased room size, number, and differentiation of rooms by usage (fig. 26); 3) increased acquisition of technologies, utilities, and household amenities (fig. 27). These patterns of room usage are each organized according to three stages of technological/industrial and social/cultural development: pre-modern, transitional, and modern. These three stages of development summarize continuity and change in room usage across time in the floor plans of America's common houses.

The three charts in figures 25, 26, and 27 depict a range of important domestic functions which could form the basis for plan interpretation and a basis for interpreting and naming common houses. For example, classifying common houses simply by recording the number and arrangement of rooms (as succinctly summarized in the term "four-square") is one of the simplest ways to understand the spatial logic of domestic function. Far more significant than exterior form or architectural style, the functional analysis of common houses offers a means of evaluation and classification that also has significance and meaning to both makers and users.

All three charts are structured by an overarching technological/social paradigm in which the entrance of industrialized methods of housing production in the late nineteenth and early twentieth centuries dramatically transformed both the making of common houses and the domestic lives of their inhabitants. Typically, these transformations resulted in the addition of improvements such as: three-fixture bathrooms, kitchen technologies, public utilities, dining rooms, private bedrooms with closets, and recreational front porches—all features unavailable to residents of common houses at the beginning of the twentieth century. Consequently, the classification of America's common houses can roughly be divided into three overlapping stages reflecting the great divide between nineteenth-century pre-modern and twentieth-century modern periods. In between, an overlapping transitional period marks the slow, incremental application of these new industrial methods and technologies into a pre-modern

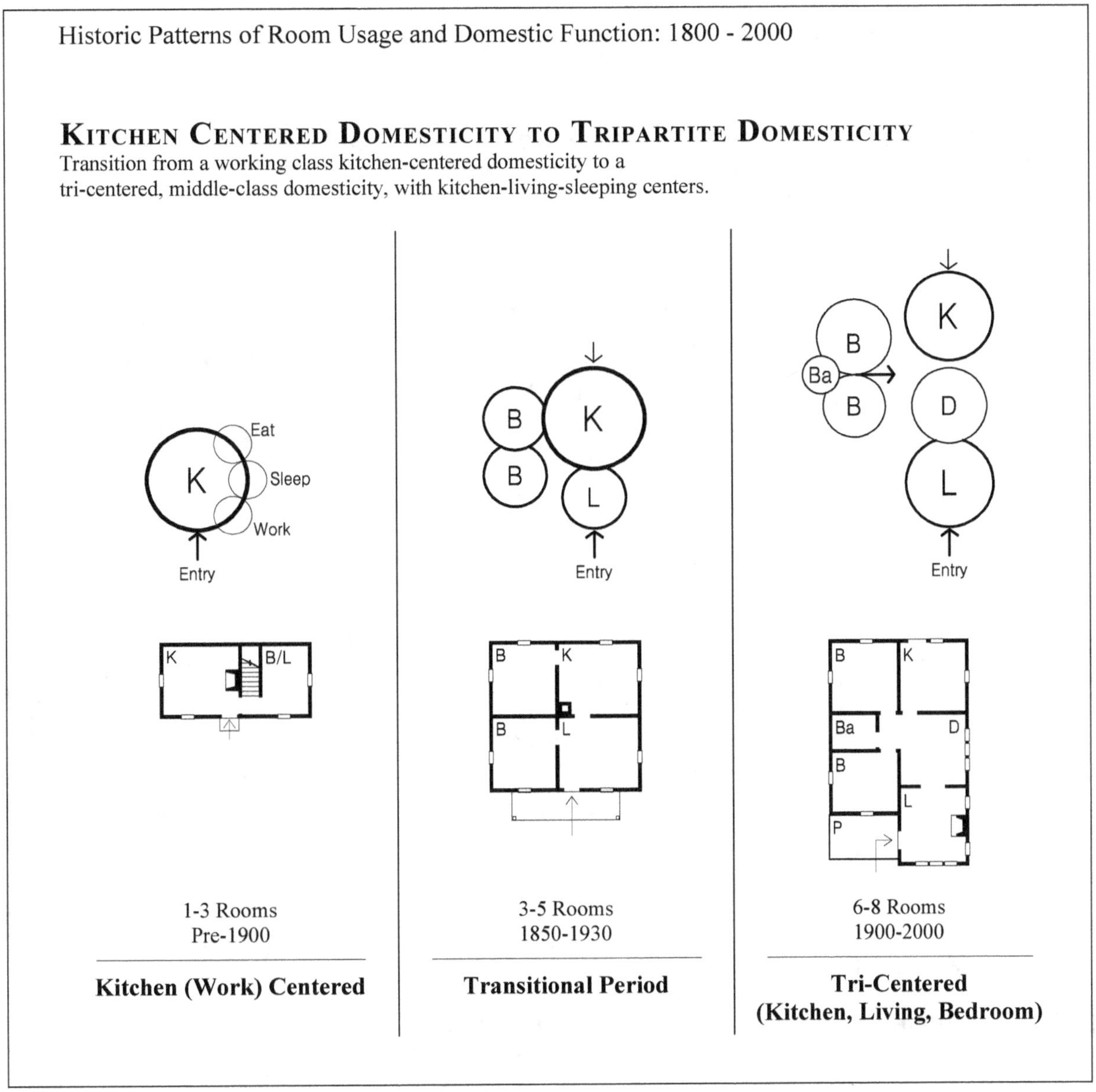

Historic Patterns of Room Usage and Domestic Function: 1800 - 2000

KITCHEN CENTERED DOMESTICITY TO TRIPARTITE DOMESTICITY

Transition from a working class kitchen-centered domesticity to a tri-centered, middle-class domesticity, with kitchen-living-sleeping centers.

1-3 Rooms	3-5 Rooms	6-8 Rooms
Pre-1900	1850-1930	1900-2000
Kitchen (Work) Centered	**Transitional Period**	**Tri-Centered (Kitchen, Living, Bedroom)**

Fig. 25. Historic patterns of room usage and domestic function, 1800–2000. Kitchen-centered domesticity to a tri-centered spatial domesticity. The transition from a working-class, kitchen-centered domesticity to a middle-class, tripartite kitchen-living-bedroom-centered domesticity.

66 | EMPHASIZING THE FLOOR PLAN

Historic Patterns of Room Usage and Domestic Function: 1800 - 2000

INCREASING DIFFERENTIATION IN ROOM USAGE AND ROOM NUMBER

Transition from a few multi-functional rooms to increased number of rooms with single-function usage. Continuous expansion for all classes all house types.

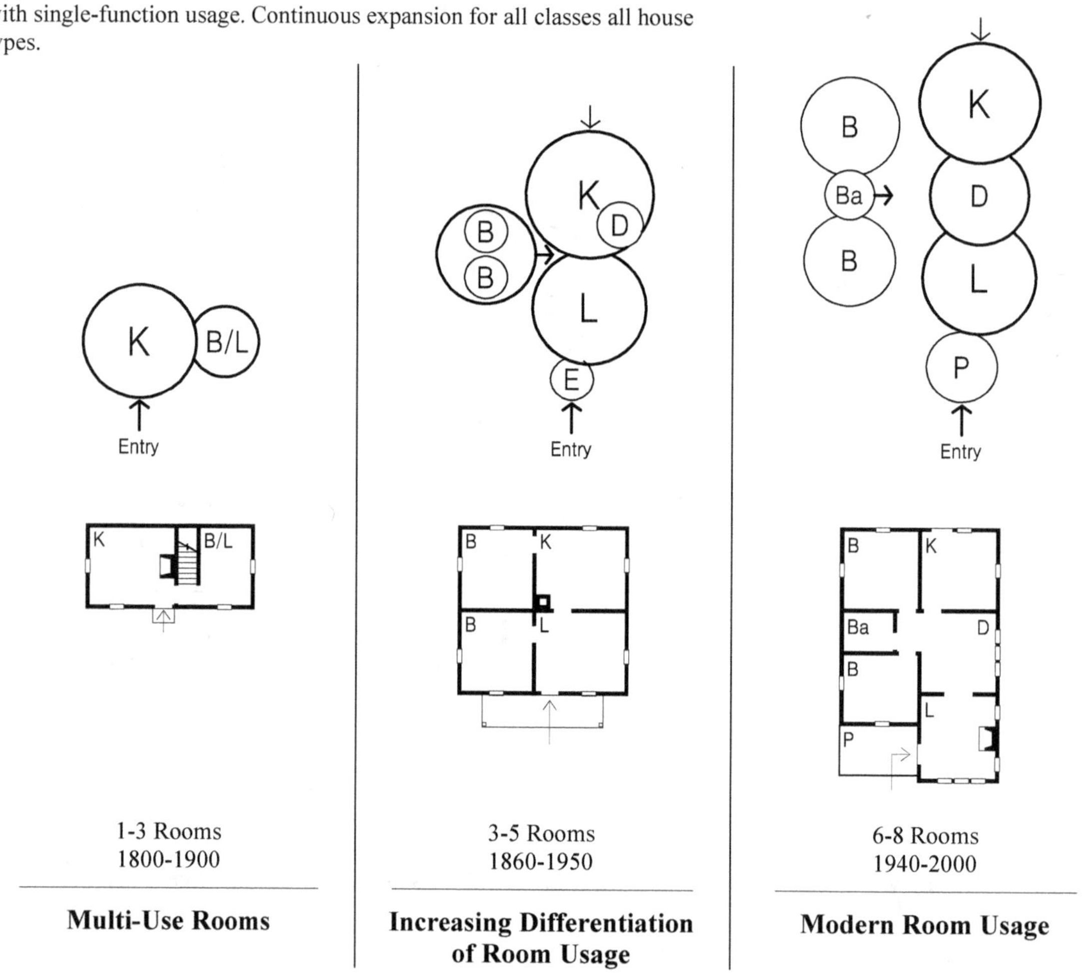

1-3 Rooms 1800-1900	3-5 Rooms 1860-1950	6-8 Rooms 1940-2000
Multi-Use Rooms	**Increasing Differentiation of Room Usage**	**Modern Room Usage**

Fig. 26. Historic patterns of room usage and domestic function, 1800–2000. Increasing number of rooms and differentiation in room usage. The transition from a working-class house with a few multi-functional rooms to a middle-class house with multiple rooms differentiated by specific functions.

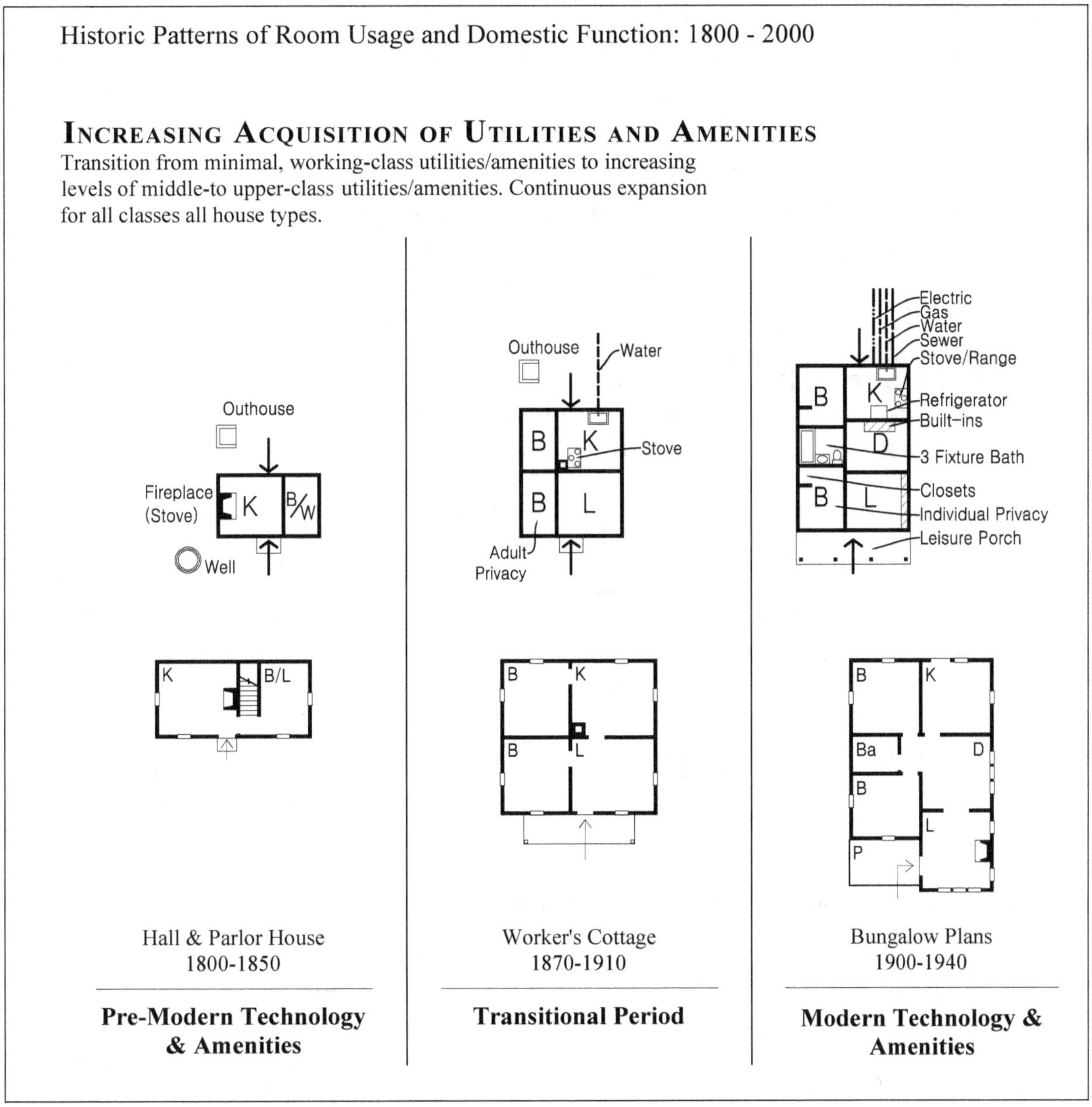

EMPHASIZING THE FLOOR PLAN | 67

Historic Patterns of Room Usage and Domestic Function: 1800 - 2000

INCREASING ACQUISITION OF UTILITIES AND AMENITIES

Transition from minimal, working-class utilities/amenities to increasing levels of middle-to upper-class utilities/amenities. Continuous expansion for all classes all house types.

Hall & Parlor House 1800-1850	Worker's Cottage 1870-1910	Bungalow Plans 1900-1940
Pre-Modern Technology & Amenities	**Transitional Period**	**Modern Technology & Amenities**

Fig. 27. Historic patterns of room usage and domestic function, 1800–2000. Increasing acquisition of utilities and amenities. The transition from a working-class domesticity with minimum utilities and amenities to a late twentieth-century domesticity offering the maximization of utilities and amenities to all classes.

house-building and domestic culture (fig. 28). This transformational period also marks the gradual emergence of a new, widening middle-class majority housing culture and a fundamental change from a previous, two-tiered class system of domestic haves and have nots. It is the emergence of this transformational middle class that is so clearly recorded in the record of common-house production during the late nineteenth and early twentieth century.⁹

Historic Stages of Domestic Improvement
The improvement of housing and domestic life in successive eras.

Pre-Modern Era, Working-Class Domesticity: 1800-1900

1) Houses of 1 to 3 rooms.
2) Kitchen centered domesticity.
3) Minimal utility technological conveniences
4) All rooms multi-purpose and containing work

Representative Houses

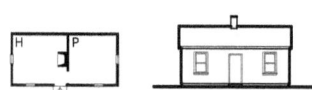

2 Rooms (Hall & Parlor Plan Types)

Transitional Era, Working-to-Middle-Class Domesticity: 1860-1930

1) Houses of 3 to 5 rooms.
2) Tri-centered domesticity: kitchen, living, bedrooms
3) Employment/work increasingly leaves the home.
4) Transitional utility & bathroom facilities (threshold between working and middle class).

4 Rooms (Four-Box Plan Types)

Modern Era, Middle-Class Domesticity: 1900-2000

1) Houses of 5 to 8 rooms (Bungalow period, 5-6 rooms; Ranch period, 7-8 rooms).
2) Tri-centered domesticity: kitchen/living/bedrooms
3) Work away from home.
4) Modern utilities and amenities.

6 Rooms (Bungalow Plan Types)

Fig. 28. Historic stages of middle-class housing and domestic development.

4
IDENTIFYING THE FLOOR PLAN FROM THE OUTSIDE

I have recommended the floor plan as a remedy for the problems of naming and classifying common houses. But, as anyone involved in housing documentation will stress, it is one thing to advocate for the importance of house plans and an entirely different matter to obtain these plans, especially for common houses. While there are occasional private, archival, and governmental sources for floor plans, the largest portion of common houses, especially for pre-1950 housing, has never been recorded in any sources. Therefore many preservationists, housing specialists, and especially state historic-preservation officials will draw a firm line at the prospect of having to enter houses to obtain floor plans, not to mention the technical skills and costs that may be required to create even basic plans. For many professionals, these objections eliminate the floor plan as a basic method of housing classification. It has been my experience that housing administrators are especially quick to condemn even the mention of the floor plan as a possible remedy for popular-housing classification even though they may personally acknowledge its advantages. These are serious issues which would seem to limit the possibility of floor plan analysis, but, as we have so often had cause to say throughout this book, it doesn't have to be that way.

Techniques for obtaining floor-plan estimates from exterior observation constitute a preliminary research method. Without such a method, it has been my experience that the initial phases of common-house research are overwhelmed by a confusion of exterior form and style analysis, leading to vaguely worded summaries of difficult-to-classify "vernacular" types. I would like to stress from the outset, however, that I am not advocating the old discredited methods of "windshield survey" implying a drive-by approach to the documentation of buildings. The ability to accurately understand the interiors of houses is just as critical to popular-housing interpretation (if not more so) as it is to traditional architectural building documentation. Nevertheless, in using a method of plan estimation from the exterior, we are acknowledging fundamental differences in the way common houses in great numbers are documented and studied from the ways traditional, individual historic buildings are studied. A specific problem of common-house study is that we often do not initially know what houses we should study or analyze in any detail. (This is a rare problem in traditional housing analysis.) In these typical situations, floor-plan estimation from the outside is an essential method of approach (*IVA*, 7-13).

Basic Rules

In order to interpret common houses, it is almost always important to understand the surrounding context of local and regional common-house types. The need for such contextual summary is fundamentally different from the documentation of high-style or unique individual houses which are often selected for documentation because they do not relate to others of their kind. This need to understand the collective context of common houses points to the reasons why plan analysis from the exterior is an important preliminary method for investigation and documentation. Unlike the study of unique uncommon houses, it is not usually clear or obvious which common houses should be studied or examined. Therefore, a method of preliminary analysis, such as reading the floor plan from the outside, is an invaluable investigative tool.

For the preliminary documentation of common houses within a survey area, it is not necessary to get inside every house or even most houses. The plan documentation process for common houses is certainly not derailed by limited access to any one house because, once the basic patterns of local floor plans are understood, considerable interpretation of interior plans can be obtained from the outside of similar houses. While at some point it is absolutely essential to verify outside observations with inside documentation, there is a great deal to be learned about the inside from the outside. Certainly there is enough information to be gathered for general survey analysis and preliminary classification. Furthermore, it is almost always possible for local and regional specialists to make highly informed evaluations of preliminary data and to access unusual and difficult-to-classify houses. Review by local specialists will help to ensure accuracy or at least to raise questions that may require further study, house visitation, and documentation.

The detailed surveys or documentation of common houses, for example through technical drawings, should only be initiated after the dominant types of common housing have been clearly identified. Following the recommendations of this book, houses selected for documentation should be the most common or typical representatives of their particular type. (Note how different this criterion is from the selection of elite historical, one-of-a-kind houses.) But, there are no established rules about the degree of documentation for common houses. Since most common houses plans are derived from and related to well-known plan prototypes, the need for elaborate documentation may be diminished, but this is new field without established standards.

What follows is an outline of specific strategies for determining house plans from exterior inspection and analysis. For both beginning observers and established professionals without plan-reading experience, the prospect of learning a new language of house plans may seem daunting. But it is not an impossible task and, like any craft, there are overarching principles and basic rules of thumb. Perhaps the most important principle is the recognition that there is almost always a limited range of recurring house types in most residential neighborhoods. Once these most common types are mastered (linking exterior forms and interior plans), the vernacular-housing landscape will become far more understandable. This is an important realization because, if each common house was significantly different from the next, as elite, high-style, architect-designed houses tend to be, the problem of plan identification from the outside would be infinitely more difficult and truly the task for experts. Fortunately this is not the case. But it is absolutely necessary to begin by determining the dominant housing types; otherwise the unfamiliar blizzard of frequently remodeled common houses will overwhelm the uninitiated. But as no veteran historian of stylistic classification would venture on to the Victorian street without a basic knowledge of the differences between the Greek Revival, Romanesque, and Queen Anne, no aficionado of popular houses would venture into the blur of the suburbs without sufficient knowledge of the basic house-plan types, including the ranch, four-square, and Cape. So study the basic plan types, and venture forth into the wily, but knowable, vernacular-housing landscape.

Fieldwork Techniques for Identifying the Floor Plan

The key to successful fieldwork is preparation. The following techniques may apply to both the documentation of individual houses and production of larger surveys for multiple houses within neighborhoods, districts, or regions (*IVA,* 21-32).

BEFORE THE SURVEY

HOMEWORK. Study the national, regional, and local literature about the house types you will be observing. Attempt to memorize, as a set, both the typical floor plans and the exterior facades of the houses you are likely to encounter. This will help you to think of a specific floor plan when you see a house in the field. Expect to find both similarities and differences between published, national examples and the local and regional types you will encounter. A consistent theme of local/regional investigations is to identify the uniqueness or variety of local/regional examples with respect to established national/regional types—this is the essence of what constitutes local and regional "vernacular" expression and can lead to the exciting, groundbreaking part of local housing research.

CONSULT KNOWLEDGEABLE LOCALS. The knowledge of local housing is rarely obtained through literature review or searching the web and most often is the result of extensive house visitation experience. A good way to quickly obtain this knowledge is to interview people with experience of local houses and house plans before beginning a survey. Often some of the most knowledgeable people have simply been inside many houses, and frequently include contractors, real estate agents, and emergency workers. Recognize, however, that just getting inside houses does not guarantee expertise about house plans or housing history—not everyone remembers plans, and few can interpret them in a wider context.

UNDERSTAND HISTORIC CHANGE. We should not automatically assume that the way houses look and function today are the same as when they were built or occupied. From outside surveys, we should always be mindful that existing facades may or may not reveal the room arrangement and domestic functions of previous users. In the most difficult situations, there is no substitute for the experience that comes from the visitation and documentation of many houses.

Surveying Houses

Preliminary reconnaissance survey. First drive around your survey area and attempt to identify the basic types of houses both within and outside the area you are documenting (*IVA,* 23-27). This is an important strategy even when documenting a single house because common houses usually achieve their contextual logic, their fit, in relation to other similar houses. Expect to find remodeled houses that might conceal an area's standard types.

Get inside dominant type houses. Attempt to visit the interiors of the most popular forms of housing in your survey area (either before, during, or after your survey). Your research assumptions about any particular house are greatly enhanced by your familiarity with similar houses. Plan identification is clearly a skill where familiarity from careful observation and house visitation breeds expertise. There is no substitute or shortcut to this housing experience, and a combination of study and fieldwork (not either/or) is the path toward understanding common houses.

Toxic exceptional houses. Do not waste time figuring out odd or exceptional houses (no matter how interesting or puzzling). This is a very important rule, both for beginners, who know only a little, and veterans, who know a lot. Too often, difficult-to-identify houses will confuse beginners and waste valuable time for experienced observers. As a rule, it is critically important to first locate and identify the dominant house types in your survey area and then proceed to identify the secondary and the tertiary types. Only when the dominant types and subtypes are thoroughly mastered should you proceed to examine the more unusual houses in your survey area. Remember that special, individual, and odd houses will stand out at the end of your survey, as they always have stood out, within a context of more uniform, common houses. Also remember that, in the field, you are likely to forget this important rule, because we are all attracted to the odd, unique, and uncommon. So learn to resist this temptation and turn your attention to the common, popular, and ordinary housing.

Common houses that change. Expect to find changes and additions to the common-house types you have studied. Remember that the exteriors and the interior plans of modest houses have frequently been changed over time—this is a basic characteristic of common houses. Therefore, train yourself to identify the underlying, original form of the common house underneath subsequent additions and remodeling changes. The ability to discover underlying unity beneath remodeling is one of the most advanced skills of exterior observation.

Rules for Floor-Plan Identification from the Exterior

Common houses typically reveal a great deal of information about their floor plans from the outside. While there is no substitute for interior house visitation, the basic plan can usually be determined from exterior analysis. For example, experienced contractors and inspectors can usually make extremely accurate predictions about floor plans by reading the many clues about the plan from the outside of the house. There are some basic rules for figuring out house plans, and with practice you can become highly skilled in this process. Soon you will amaze friends and frighten your neighbors with your ability to see through walls and reveal the inner workings of houses you have never visited. But to begin, the most important thing to do is to become familiar with as many types of local plans as possible through observation, research, interview, and house visitation. Although the quantity of common houses is immense, the vast majority of residential neighborhoods demonstrate a consistent unity of a limited range of floor plans. In fact, the more common and modest the house, the more likely it is to obey uniform rules for its floor plan.

To begin, you will usually be looking at the front facade of a house with perhaps views of both sides. Access to a view of the back side (or all facades) is very helpful but not absolutely necessary. If you are a beginner, you probably will need some kind of notepad to remember observations and to make a rough preliminary sketch of the plan. A digital camera is a lifesaver for beginner and expert alike. To begin the viewing process, ask yourself some basic questions, like, "Where's the kitchen?"

Where's the Kitchen?

Locating the kitchen is probably the single most important goal for understanding the plan of the common house. And this is true worldwide. Although interpreting window organization provides far more information, locating the kitchen reveals the primary relationships of room arrangement and domestic function for common houses. Conversely, if you fail to locate the kitchen or initially misinterpret its location from the outside, the likelihood of completely misinterpreting the plan is greatly increased.

Unfortunately the kitchen is most often located on the private back of common-house types, making exact location from the public front sometimes impossible. There is a hidden advantage to this problem, however, because even if you can not determine the exact location of the kitchen from the front side, the process of rehearsing where the kitchen might be located will take you through a good checklist of the critical spatial relationships fundamental to almost all common houses. The kitchen is located at the functional heart of the typical house, increasingly so for older and smaller working-class houses. This is the functional domestic "logic" of the kitchen. So think about the kitchen, even though it might not seem like the logical place to start, and you will begin to understand the essential logic of the common-house plan and its domestic function.

Fig. 29. Locating the kitchen from the outside. A door on the driveway side of the house almost always leads to the kitchen. Over-the-sink kitchen windows are raised and shortened. A vent stack, a small pipe on the roof, often locates the kitchen sink. Box-ranch (four-box plan), Springfield, Oregon.

Fortunately there are many other clues to locating the kitchen from the outside of the house (fig. 29). The typical location for the kitchen is on the back or driveway side. Alerting you to the location of this back/side kitchen are several basic exterior features. A back door almost always enters the kitchen or a service space adjacent to the kitchen, so locate this door. This typical pattern changes in attached-garage houses like the ranch where the "back door" is concealed and usually enters the kitchen from the garage or a service room adjacent to the garage. There are only a few exceptions to this basic rule of back-door kitchen entry. For example, there are other exterior back doors sometimes entering the dining room, like a patio sliding door in a larger ranch house or screen-door entries into porches, and there are often second back doors into larger houses. When a door is located on the side of the house opening onto a driveway, this door almost always enters the kitchen or leads to the kitchen through a kitchen service space or stairway adjacent to the kitchen.

There are other clues to kitchen location: (1) A window above or near the kitchen sink is a very common feature for houses after 1900. From the outside, the kitchen window, similar to the bathroom window is one of the smallest, shortest windows in a house. Kitchens and bathrooms can therefore be confused from the outside. Generally the kitchen window is wider than the bathroom and may be a double window. (2) A thin vent stack (a small chimney pipe on the roof) often locates the sewer gas ventilation pipe from the kitchen sink, but it can also be confused with a bath or lavatory vent stack. Therefore, vent pipes on the roof may identify either the kitchen or the bath. (3) Kitchens are located on the back ground floor of most single-family houses, with a few significant exceptions, such as ranches with kitchens on the front, street side. (4) Electric meters are often located near the kitchen, which is often the room with the greatest electrical consumption. (5) Today, special pop-out, fishbowl windows and personalized items like chimes and thermometers often mark the kitchen or kitchen-dining area on the outside.

Windows: Keys to Room Location and Function

By any standard, the ability to interpret windows by their type, shape, and size, like seeing into a person's soul through their eyes, is the most important key for understanding the room and plan organization of a house. Because the major types of common houses have recognizable patterns of size, shape, and location, you should learn to memorize the standard configuration of windows in the houses you are studying. Some windows are signature elements of their house types and can be recognized nationally. For example, the large picture window of the early ranch house living room is a well-known symbol of the suburban lifestyle. While most windows do not reveal the identity of their rooms so consistently, a dwelling's total window configuration is the single most important factor for revealing considerable information about the floor plan and its domestic function. Before 1900, however, and increasingly before the Civil War, pre-industrial windows were typically built in more uniform sizes, making room usage assessments from window size and shape more difficult.

Fig. 30. Exterior windows, the key to identifying the interior floor plan and room usage. The rooms in this split-level house from Union, New Jersey, follow a standard pattern. The large picture window with side lights locates the living room. Two equal, medium-sized windows above the garage locate the two smaller bedrooms. Horizontal windows within the overhead door locate the garage. A small special window beside the front door locates an entrance area or storage room.

Though windows come in all sizes, there are relationships between window type, size, shape, and location that are consistent markers of room usage in many different types of houses (fig. 30). Generally the largest window or largest string of multiple windows locates the living room, which is also the largest room in most houses. Medium-sized windows usually locate the medium-sized rooms, typically dining rooms and bedrooms. Smaller windows usually reveal smaller rooms such as baths, pantries, closets, and entries. Kitchen windows are built in various sizes, medium to small. A window over the sink has been a standard for many house types for the last hundred years, except in minimum kitchens such as galley kitchens in apartments. Small, specialized windows, like an octagon, may mark the entry, and very small windows may locate special rooms or areas like closets, attics, and entries. Basement windows have been thin and horizontal in most houses from the beginning of their appearance.

Special windows in various shapes and sizes appear in different stylistic periods and offer a consistent way to understand regional house plans. For example, small, paired stained glass windows raised on either side of an exposed or concealed fireplace/chimney consistently mark the living room of a bungalow or craftsman-era living room. The location of the stairway, always a key to understanding the floor plan in two-story houses, but always a problem to locate from the outside, is often signaled by a window located midway between first-floor and second-floor windows.

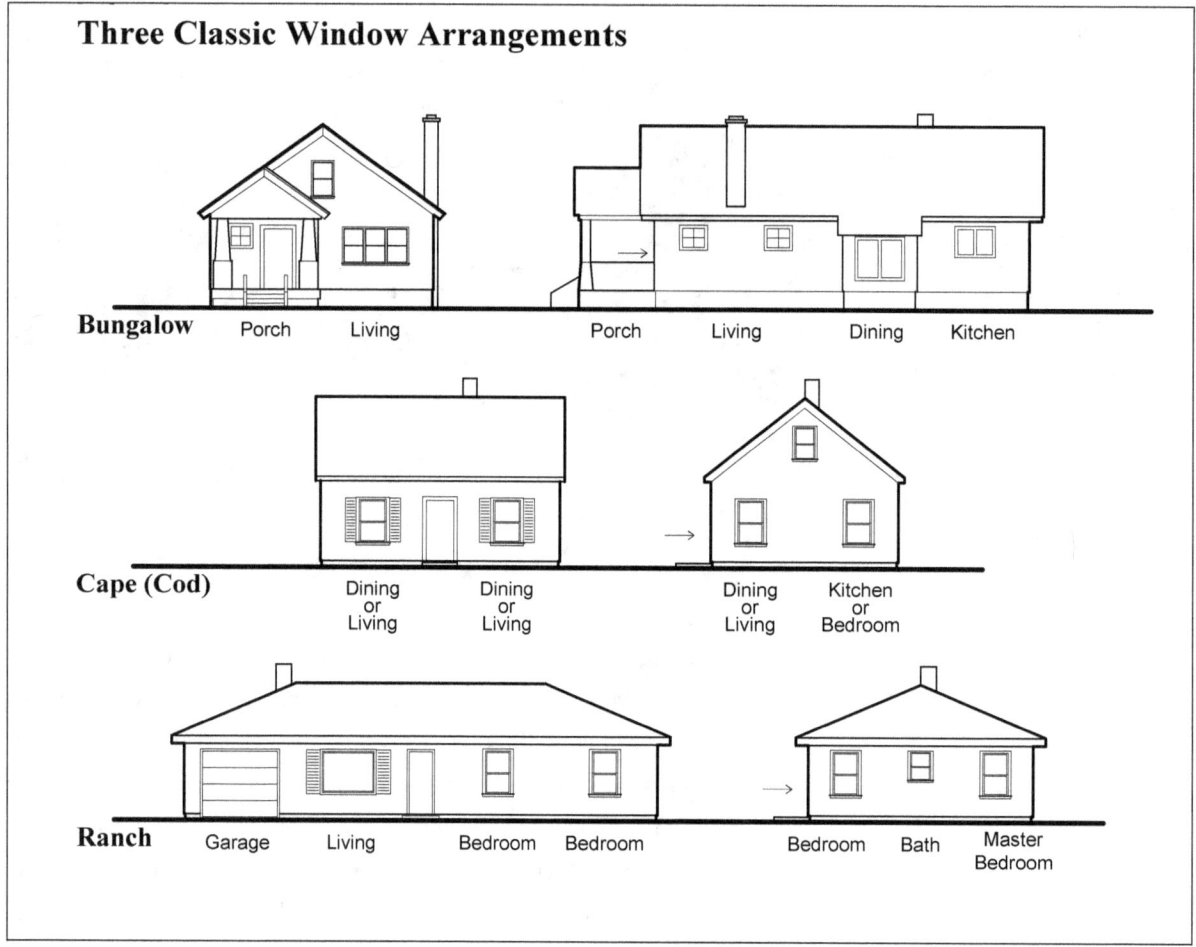

Fig. 31. Three classic patterns of window arrangement: bungalow house, Cape (Cod) house, ranch house.

Once you understand the generic vocabulary of windows signaling room locations, you will begin to understand common groups or patterns of windows that are characteristic of different house types in different historical eras. There are consistent and unmistakable nationally recognized patterns of window groupings for common houses. For example, the sequence of different types of windows identifying the living room, dining room, and kitchen along the side of the classic bungalow; or the window, door, and garage openings of a classic ranch; or the strict symmetry of windows on either side of the Cape (Cod) front door (fig. 31). These classic iconic symbols of popular housing deserve to take their place in the pantheon of classic American houses alongside the more widely recognized forms of high-style houses, like the ribbon casement windows in Frank Lloyd Wright's Prairie Houses or the second-story Palladian window of two-story Georgian houses of the Colonial period.

Other Exterior Features for Interpreting the Plan

Exterior Doors. An American standard is the dual-centered and dual-entered house with kitchen and living-room centers. Announcing this duality on the outside of almost all single-family houses are two doors that typically lead to either the kitchen or the living room in all but the smallest houses, apartments, and early trailers. Houses with one exterior door include small pre-1900 houses with one and two rooms, and most apartments in multi-story buildings. Complicating this typical pattern of two-door domesticity are kitchen doors concealed from the outside by garages, as well as three and more doors in houses of increasing upper-middle-class size and wealth.

Chimneys. The location of the chimney(s) is sometimes helpful to understanding the house plan. Two common locations for chimneys are either on the perimeter of the house or near the center of the roof. Remember that almost all chimneys are located along a wall and not in the center of a room, which helps locate interior walls from the outside. Multiple chimneys may identify multi-unit houses or, for example, in the case of the bungalow, two chimneys may identify the furnace (usually near the center) and the living-room fireplace (often on the perimeter). Multiple flues, visible as chimney pots or stacks on the top of the chimney, may indicate the combination of furnace and fireplace flues or multi-unit apartments.

Utilities. The location of utilities on the outside of a house is highly variable, but sometimes they are important indicators for room usage. As already mentioned, roof vent-stacks exhausting sewer gas are important markers for locating both kitchens and bathrooms. Gas meters are usually located near the front, street side of the house, and the number of both gas and electric meters is a telltale sign of multiple-unit residencies. Electric-meter locations are variable but are often located close to the kitchen in common houses.

Personal artifacts. Curtains, decorative lighting, and personal items are often gathered around the kitchen windows and kitchen doorway. Kitchen windows over sinks are often the collectors of personal items on display. A glance at a house during the evening when it is illuminated by interior lighting can reveal much about the plan, but it is not suggested that research be conducted in this manner.

Duplexes and multi-unit houses. Twin doors on the front facade of a house are one of the most consistent indicators of a duplex (although

Fig. 32. Identifying the duplex from the outside. Side-by-side twin doors and similarly scaled and aligned first- and second-floor windows are classic signs of the duplex. Standard duplex ("two-flat"), Milwaukee, Wisconsin.

there are many duplexes with only one, common front door). Other duplex indicators include double or multiple mailboxes, street numbers, doorbells, gas meters, garbage cans, and parking spaces (fig. 32). The one-over-one duplex, one America's most popular multi-unit houses, can be recognized nationally when the windows of first and second floor line up and are identical in size on both floors. Likewise, when the windows of a two-story house are irregular top-to-bottom and do not align, this most often identifies a one-family, middle-class house, although it could have been converted to a duplex.

Strategies for Interpreting Difficult-to-Identify Houses

If you get bogged down trying to understand difficult-to-interpret houses, remember one of the most important rules for interpreting common housing: "Unusual houses do not disprove the basic rules of common houses." Exceptional houses are merely expected exceptions to the larger consistent rules of popular-housing identification. A corollary is: "Consistency and unity prove the basic rules of popular house identification." Both rules are important to remember because, in normal experience, it is typical to linger over unusual or unique houses. This is what most of us have been culturally trained to do. So, as we have emphasized, expect to be attracted to unique houses, and then train yourself to move on to the next common house!

While a few houses are truly unique, many more unfamiliar houses are actually familiar house types that have been remodeled to become, on the outside or inside, radically changed. This is, vernacularly, quite normal and is to be expected. The major problem for beginners during initial observation, however, is that you might not recognize a heavily remodeled familiar type of house. More experienced observers, however, quickly recognize the consistent characteristics of remodeled houses behind radically altered facades. Like any other skill, interpreting common, popular, vernacular, everyday houses requires observation and practice. The consistent organization is out there; we just have to find it.

Finally, remember that house-plan identification from the outside is just one of the tools of analysis, like Sanborn Maps, census reports, historical photos, interviews, and building records, for investigating America's common residential landscape. As one of these tools, it is only a preliminary survey device that must be combined with more accurate data such as house visitation and the standard methods of documentation (see *IVA*, 19-43). Nevertheless, despite its limitations, house-plan survey from the exterior is an extremely useful method of investigating common houses. Without adequate methods of classification and nomenclature, common residential environments will remain marginalized and difficult-to-analyze landscapes of anonymous houses. But it doesn't have to be that way.

5
Houses with Names: Interpreting America's Common Houses

Three overarching themes about the current status of housing nomenclature and classification have guided this study: (1) the inadequacy of current methods of exterior-style and exterior-form classification to interpret the vast majority of American's common housing; (2) the need for a revised method of interior, floor-plan classification to improve current methods, and (3) the need for a census-based survey to determine a dominant house-type classification for common houses.

While the current methods of interpretation are criticized, they need not be replaced but only modified so that a broader, more complete spectrum of common dwellings might be included for interpretation. My principal recommendation, for the inclusion of floor-plan-based classification, could be standardized to produce a two-part, exterior (style/form) and interior (plan/function) formula for common-house identification. While not required for classifying upper-class houses with adequate names, the addition of a more plan-based interpretation is essential for classifying common houses.

Simple Strategies for Getting Started

As we have seen, the houses you thought were simple and ordinary are actually more nuanced and richly layered than you might have imagined. I hope I've allowed you to appreciate this complexity, but I also hope that I haven't overemphasized their complexity to the point that we cannot interpret them for ourselves. To promote their accessibility, I would like to conclude with a few simple case studies about how houses in your neighborhood might be classified and named. I hope these examples might set a tone for future study and provide a template for local efforts to understand and appreciate common houses. This process could begin by simply examining the houses outside your front door or across town or in any residential environment.

Figure 33 shows the title page and a four-page section on the ranch house from a small booklet about the common houses of Springfield, Oregon. It was compiled by my students from the Historic Preservation Program at the University of Oregon. From a survey of the oldest portion of the city, the booklet attempts to name and classify Springfield's most popular or dominant types of housing.

Since Springfield is a twentieth-century western city, the American ranch house figures prominently in its housing history, and I include that portion of the booklet in figure 33. Through a census of the district's housing types, my students determined that there were three dominant types of ranch house out of hundreds of ranches in the survey area, including several other less numerous subtypes. Following the advice outlined in this book, each major numerical type was then analyzed through exterior photos and interior plans and, following local investigation and interviews, given a name. (Usually, since there are seldom any standard, well-known names, several names are listed.)

Each house type was than analyzed for basic characteristics, like the typical number of rooms and type of plan organization, and a summary text was written to define the local-house type within a context of similar houses on a regional and national scale. This summary description of a common local-house type is always difficult to write because, as we have seen, there is so little information about the most popular forms of common housing.

The complete booklet describes the full range of Springfield's housing. The ranch house examples were selected because, although familiar to most readers as one of America's most popular house types, two of Springfield's most popular versions of the ranch might not found in your neighborhood—the "kitchen-in-the-front ranch" and the small "box-ranch." As we have stressed, it is the occurrence of these local variations of national house types that is one of the keys (and joys) of common-house survey and research.

Although not a definitive study, I believe the booklet's sample pages and simple format summarize the basic categories of information and analysis critical to the evaluation and classification of common houses. It is not a tabulation that requires advanced degrees, but it does require determination for counting all the houses in a survey area and persistence in attempting to find a dominant underlying order in houses that may not appear so orderly on first inspection. Despite these difficulties, we can also

Fig. 33. (opposite through page 87) Interpreting Springfield, Oregon's dominant types of ranch houses. From the booklet *Everyday Houses: A Guide to Springfield's Most Popular House Types, 1880–1980.*

EVERYDAY HOUSES

A Guide to Springfield's Most Popular House Types
1880-1980

The Ranch
c. 1950-1980

The Ranch became popular in the 1950s and replaced smaller World War II era housing. By the 1970s, the ranch house had become Springfield and America's most popular housing type. The increasing popularity and use of the automobile played a significant role in the development of the Ranch, which incorporated carports and garages into the main body of the house. The impact of the automobile is reflected in many features of the house. For example, the traditional front door sidewalk connects to the driveway rather than directly to the street as it had done in previous house types. Ranch houses are recognized by their broad one-story façades with very low-pitched roofs. The plan of a typical ranch house is divided into three functional zones: car area, living area, and bedroom area.

Standard Ranch | Kitchen-in-Front Ranch | Box Ranch

Springfield's Ranch houses can be divided into three basic types: the Standard Ranch, and the Kitchen-in-Front Ranch, and Box Ranch.

Standard Ranch

ALSO KNOWN AS THE AMERICAN RANCH, SUBURBAN TRACT HOUSE, OR RANCH

c.1950-1980

1165 6TH STREET

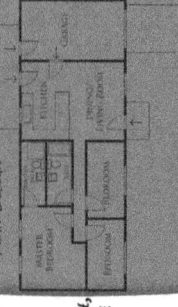

855 "D" STREET

TYPICAL FLOOR PLAN DESIGN

Common Floor Plan Elements:
- Six-room 1st floor plan
- Rectangular-shaped plan
- Three-part plan: garage, bedrooms & public areas
- Little to no front porch
- Single story in height

The Standard Ranch typically consists of a simple rectangular plan that positions itself parallel to the street. In its simplest form, the plan consists of a centrally located living room, dining room, and kitchen with the garage and bedrooms located on either side. Unlike any other previous house type, the ranch had a fully attached garage that commonly consumed 20% to 30% of the volume of the house. Ranches have been built all across the country and are the most common type of housing in America today—as it is also Springfield's most popular type.

Kitchen-in-Front Ranch

Also known as an American Ranch, Suburban Tract House, or a Ranch

c. 1950-1980

735 4TH STREET

439 8TH STREET

The Kitchen-in-Front Ranch is a sub-type of the popular Standard Ranch. While the Standard Ranch's kitchen was usually placed along the back of the house facing the backyard, the Kitchen-in-Front Ranch positioned its kitchen along the front, street-side of the dwelling. In this configuration, the bedrooms and living room were placed along the backside of the house. In Springfield, Kitchen-in-Front Ranches are very popular and are often recognized by the presence of small windows between the front door and the garage and by the absence of a large picture window that most often showcases the living room on the front of the house.

TYPICAL FLOOR PLAN DESIGN

Common Floor Plan Elements:
- Six-room 1st floor plan
- Rectangular-shaped plan
- Three-part plan: garage, bedrooms & public areas
- Little to no front porch
- Single story in height

Box Ranch

Also known as an American Ranch, a Suburban Tract House, or a Ranch

c.1950-1980

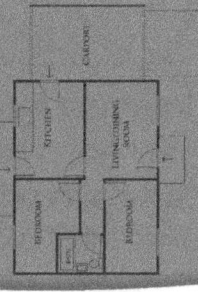

1084 "D" STREET

TYPICAL 1ST FLOOR PLAN

Although similar to the Standard Ranch, the Box Ranch is a smaller, more modest version of the typical ranch. It is more square in plan shape and often has an attached carport instead of a fully enclosed garage. Box ranches may also have the same floorplan of a small Standard Ranch, but without a garage.

Common Floor Plan Elements:
- Five-room 1st floor plan
- Square-shaped plan
- Three-part plan: garage, bedrooms & public areas
- Single story in height

be assured that consistent organizing patterns do in fact underlie the common houses we encounter in our communities—we just have to discover that organization.

Interpreting America's Common Houses

While better names and meaningful classification has been our goal, the larger purpose of this book is to promote the understanding and appreciation of common houses and their role in the development of American domestic culture. The floor plan has been emphasized as a potentially useful vehicle for understanding the historic patterns of daily domestic life. However, although one of the major goals of housing research is the interpretation of domestic life, we primarily study the container, not the domestic life itself. Interpreting house plans for traces of design intent and the record of human activity is the difficult task of material-cultural analysis. This study of bricks and boards to reveal human intention and activity is certainly not a privileged substitute for the standard methods of historical analysis and social science. Nevertheless, house-plan interpretation can be a powerful tool for revealing broad historic patterns of domesticity and culture that would be difficult to obtain through other methods of analysis.

In the case of common houses, the historical development of floor plans reveals an overall unity of a limited range of basic types. By any standard of comparison, these plans are far more unified and less individualized than equivalent middle- to upper-class houses. The patterns of domestic culture revealed in the study of common houses and their floor plans are not uniform, but there are some core characteristics of the way common houses have been made and inhabited that provide insights into their function for their inhabitants.

A Context of Constraints

Although I have attempted to make simple common houses more accessible and understandable, there are still considerable constraints to basic interpretation. For example, rather than an opportunistic context of upper-class housing production, the making and inhabitation of common housing should rather be understood in a more circumscribed context of constraints. These include, most prominently, economic limitations but also the cultural constraints of social class and everyday life, reinforcing a generally tighter margin for spatial expression and error in house design and construction (fig. 34). These are the constraints of domestic life that define the more limited palette of choices in the indirect decision-making process between builders and users in the production of common houses.

We have no proper way to describe these constraints imposed by the typical speculative consumer relationship between dominant local builders and unknown, subordinate users in the production of common houses. This is especially true for the smallest, most inexpensive types of houses. Nor do we have a proper aesthetic means or anthropological vision

Fig. 34. Constraints: minimal-traditional house (four-box plan), Brownsville, Oregon.

for interpreting the "uniform" housing "selection" of this largest class of citizens who, all things being equal, might genuinely appreciate living in houses similar to their neighbors. Properly understood, these constraining perspectives from working- to middle-class users might help explain some of the seemingly "mindless," "cookie-cutter" decisions that have so often been attributed to seemingly unthinking and uncaring common-house builders and users.

Repetition and Conformity

It may still be hard for some readers to resist a negative interpretation of the repetitive conformity of common residential environments. Yet the overwhelming experience for most Americans, as well as from most people worldwide, has been to live in communities where broad housing unity (with minor degrees of individual expression), not diversity, is the overwhelming pattern. Housing conformity on this universal scale does not occur because of the calculated designs of government bureaucrats, sinister bankers, or conspiring builder/developer/realtors. Inasmuch as we can summarize the cultural production of common domestic environments, this unity is a product of a broad-based consensus about the matter-of-fact normalcy of residential communities sharing similar kinds of houses (fig. 35).

Fig. 35. Repetition: two-up, two-down (plan) houses, Homestead, Pennsylvania.

What is so difficult to articulate within the current climate of hyper-individuality and avant-guardism is the possibility that all kinds of people with varying degrees of choice, from none to unlimited, might actually prefer to live in communities sharing similar kinds of "repetitive" houses, as most people have done worldwide in almost all class cultures, except, and only occasionally, the very rich. The facts on the ground overwhelming indicate that it is culturally normal and generally acceptable to live in houses that are pretty much uniform and, in varying degrees, similar to each other. But, in the United States today, you rarely perceive this current and historical unity when you interview users, or seek the advice of professionals, or examine the dominant narratives in the vast literature of housing. Coming to terms with both the surface and underlying unity of common residential environments is not a glamorous, sexy topic, but its study is essential if we are to grasp the context of housing and domestic environments for a vast majority of Americans.

Modest Increments of Change

Most common houses are closely related in local and regional development, and their differences are generally quite modest. If you are accustomed to observing larger high-style houses, you might have to adjust your vision and expectations in order to understand the subtle differences between these common houses, for example, as we have seen in the differences between the Milwaukee houses in figure 21. At first glance, there is not much difference between these three different houses. But that is the point, because within the world of common houses, these small differences, usually unobserved in elite review, make all the difference in the world.

Similarly, in historical perspective, there are only a few basic ways to organize the rooms in houses with three, four, and five rooms to accomplish the basic tasks of domestic life (fig. 36). While modest by the standards of upper -and middle-class construction, the slight differences between these plans define the strategic playing field of popular house-design decision-making and usage. For example, within the modest limits of houses with either two-to-three rooms or four-to-five rooms are condensed the dramatic fault lines between a late-medieval and an early modern domesticity.

Fig. 36. Changes: side-hall plan with rear additions.

Likewise, throughout the history of common-house development, small, seemingly insignificant shifts in layout and construction have had major impacts on the quality of domestic life. For example, the making of bedrooms with or without closets, or the incremental addition of bathroom fixtures, or bedroom locations that allow greater privacy—these are the palette of common-house developments that signal the major shifts in standards and quality of domestic life. For the residents of common houses, these are the small, seldom recorded changes and seemingly minor adjustments in household technologies and building plan, not the articulation of a few Queen Anne details on the facade, that define the great watersheds of design decision-making and domestic usage. In the evaluation of common houses, we would do well to pay attention to these modest increments of permanence and change if we are to interpret these dwellings from the everyday perspectives of their inhabitants.

Egalitarian Principles and Common Housing

Clearly there is a need for better ways to classify and name America's common housing (fig. 37). But on how to obtain that improvement there is little agreement, especially if we attempt to interpret and classify all common houses. Even to assess all the houses on a single street or neighborhood is difficult enough, not to mention a city, a region, or a national survey. Invariably the sheer number of houses will sow confusion. Unique examples will distract. Familiar categories will become unfamiliar in local execution, and the way houses change over time will add to the general confusion. These are the standard difficulties of common-house interpretation and appreciation.

Therefore, in these situations, in order to include all houses, even the most common, we should try to maintain egalitarian principles—and the most essential is, "All houses are created equal." Of course, we also know that houses are vastly unequal in all the ways that dwellings differ in size, style, expense, age, ownership, symbolism, upkeep, and social worth. But we could also learn to look at these different kinds of houses, as we have learned to look at different kinds of people, as sharing an underlying equality. In the case of houses, it is an equality based on their basic domestic function—a commonality of internal usage uniting houses and families small and large, modest and wealthy, renter and owner. And we can make

Fig. 37. Common houses, West Allis, Wisconsin.

these egalitarian observations while simultaneously recognizing the many differences between houses, just as we have learned to do with people. So, when you are driving down another street of little bald-headed-stepchildren-like houses, those houses without names, remember: it doesn't have to be that way.

Notes

1. Houses without Names

1. Current housing estimates are extrapolated from U.S. Census Bureau, "American Housing Survey for the United States: 2005" (Current Housing Reports). Historical estimates are derived from case studies in survey areas and especially Mason C. Doan, *American Housing Production, 1880–2000: A Concise History* (Lanham, MD, 1997), xiii–xv, 143–57, and throughout.

2. The definition of vernacular architecture, including common houses used here, closely follows Thomas Carter and Elizabeth Collins Cromley, *Invitation to Vernacular Architecture* (Knoxville, TN, 2005), 7–13. Other definitions influencing this research include Henry Glassie, *Vernacular Architecture* (Bloomington, IN, 2000), 1–20, and Amos Rapoport, *House Form and Culture* (Englewood Cliffs, NJ, 1969), 1–17. Typically, definitions of vernacular architecture have emphasized the contrast and separation between elite, high-style and a common, folk architecture. Such definitions do not adequately address industrialized, suburban, and current vernaculars of the twentieth century, including the largest portion of housing lying between the extremes of elite, architect-designed housing and rural, pre-industrial forms of common housing. For American housing, this middle ground includes the major portions of working-to-middle-class, industrialized housing. For various historic reasons outlined throughout this book, there has been little agreement or study about how to name and classify this majority of houses. For revised definitions of the vernacular see Howard Davis, *The Culture of Building* (London, 2006), 3–21, and Kingston Wm. Heath, *Vernacular Architecture and Regional Design* (Amsterdam, 2009), 2–21.

3. The estimate of three-fourths (or 75 percent) of common houses is based on a review of research and case studies of current and historical housing through fieldwork in sample neighborhoods from twenty-six metropolitan areas throughout the United States. (See chapter 1, note 5, chapter 2, notes 10 and 13.) The estimation of the numbers and percentages of "common" houses compared to all other houses will be

further developed in chapter 2, where interpreting the speculative design method will be a key to this interpretation.

4. The differences between common/repetitive housing versus individualized/unique housing will be emphasized throughout this book. This distinction emphasizes the anonymity and repetition of industrialized design and speculative construction methods of local builders which increased during the second half of the nineteenth century. This new scale of mass commodity production and consumption has not received adequate historical analysis but can be gleaned from the collective record of common-house production, as outlined for example in Mary Ellen Hayward, *Baltimore's Alley Houses: Homes for Working People since the 1780s* (Baltimore, 2008), and Donna J. Rilling, *Making Houses, Crafting Capitalism, Builders in Philadelphia, 1790–1850* (Philadelphia, 2001). Although not addressing the production of housing, Lizabeth A. Cohen, *Making a New Deal: Industrial Workers in Chicago, 1919–1939* (Cambridge, UK, 1990), 99–158, provides a useful framework, in the chapter "Encountering Mass Culture," for interpreting popular consumer consumption that might be applied to the production of common houses.

5. The historical development of speculative construction methods for the vast majority of small-scale American builders has not received adequate study. Speculative building practices are broadly outlined in Sam Bass Warner, *Streetcar Suburbs: The Process of Growth in Boston (1870–1900)*, 67–116. The speculative production practices of large-scale builder-developers are more frequently analyzed, such as the Levitt family in Richard Longstreth, "The Levitts, Mass-Produced Houses, and Community Planning in the Mid-twentieth Century," in *Second Suburb: Levittown, Pennsylvania,* ed. Dianne Harris (Pittsburgh, 2010), 123–74; the developer, S. E. Gross of Chicago, in Ann Durkin Keating, *Building Chicago: Suburban Developers and the Creation of a Divided Metropolis* (Chicago, 2002), 70–88; and the developer profession in Marc A. Weiss, *The Rise of the Community Builders: The American Real Estate Industry and Urban Land Planning* (New York, 1987), 1–90.

6. For the last thirty-five years, America's vernacular architecture scholarship, including housing, has been cataloged and sponsored by the Vernacular Architecture Forum in serial publications, *Perspectives in Vernacular Architecture* and *Buildings & Landscapes,* and, for thirty years,

recent works of vernacular scholarship have been thoroughly listed in the society's *Vernacular Architecture Newsletter, VAN.*

7. For an overview of the standard nomenclature based on traditional external stylistic criteria, see Virginia and Lee McAlester, *A Field Guide to American Houses* (New York, 1992). For naming the full range of the most numerous common houses, there are no standard sources or definitions, as provided, for example, in Carl Lounsbury's regional study, *An Illustrated Glossary of Early Southern Architecture and Landscape* (New York, 1994). Perhaps the most influential, current listings of housing nomenclature are contained in National Park Service's historic preservation guidelines interpreted by State Historic Preservation Offices (SHPOs). While most SHPOs' nomenclature and classifications are still primarily based on older patterns of stylistic evaluation, there are currently efforts to reform these practices. Over the last fifteen years, I have addressed the issue of housing nomenclature in over one-hundred lectures at town meetings, neighborhood groups, schools, and historical societies throughout the country. I have had the opportunity to inquire about local housing and nomenclature, especially the difficulties of using academic or national terms to describe local or regional housing. I encourage the use of local/regional nomenclature to help define the variations of national types and terminology.

8. The dominant works of late nineteenth-century and early twentieth-century architectural scholarship still define the modern standards for architectural stylistic classification, as outlined by Summerson, *The Classical Language of Architecture*; Henry-Russell Hitchcock, *Architecture: Nineteenth and Twentieth Centuries* (Harmondsworth, Middlesex, UK, 1987); and Banister Fletcher, *A History of Architecture* (London, 1987). The inadequacy of these elite works to define common American housing developments, especially in the twentieth century, while widely recognized, has not produced alternative methods of classification and nomenclature.

9. Dell Upton, "Pattern Books and Professionalism: Aspects of the Transformation of Domestic Architecture in American, 1800–1860," in *Winterthur Portfolio* 19, nos. 2–3 (Summer–Autumn, 1984): 107–50. For excellent accounts of builders working in this pre-industrial period, see Catherine Bishir, "Jacob W. Holt: An American Builder," *Winterthur*

Portfolio 16, no. 1 (Spring 1981): 1–31, and Ritchie Garrison, *Two Carpenters: Architecture and Building in Early New England, 1799–1859* (Knoxville, 2006), 15–74.

10. For a summary of the nineteenth- and twentieth-century Colonial Revival, see Richard Guy Wilson, *Colonial Revival House* (New York, 2004). For a review of Colonial Revival house types, see Alan Gowans, *The Comfortable House: North American Suburban Architecture, 1890–1930* (Cambridge, MA, 1986), 139–65.

11. Dell Upton outlines this transformation in the production of American housing in "Pattern Books and Professionalism," 107–50. While Upton concentrates on the growth of the architectural profession and not the role of common builders, he identifies the fundamental transformation to new types and styles of building occurring at mid-century. There are no uniform definitions for identifying these new forms of difficult-to-classify industrialized housing, including popular upper-middle-class houses, ranging in size from large side-hall dwellings to smaller worker's cottages that by 1900 would include the vast majority of the nation's housing. These new, difficult-to-classify by style, middle-to upper-class houses are analyzed in Herbert Gottfried and Jan Jennings, *American Vernacular Buildings and Interiors* (New York, 2009), and Gowans, *The Comfortable House*. For new types of working-class houses, see Joseph C. Bigott, *From Cottage to Bungalow: Houses and the Working Class in Metropolitan Chicago, 1869–1929* (Chicago, 2001).

12. Fred B. Kniffen, "Folk Housing: Key to Diffusion," *Annals of the Association of American Geographers* 55, no. 4 (December 1965): 549–77, and Fred B. Kniffen and Henry Glassie, "Building in Wood in the Eastern United States: A Time-Place Perspective," *Geographical Review* 56, no. 1 (January 1966): 40–66. (Both works combine form/massing and plan classification.) Other vernacular housing surveys that primarily rely on exterior form/massing criteria include John Jakle, Robert W. Bastian, and Douglas K. Meyer, *Common Houses in America's Small Towns* (Athens, GA, 1989); Lester Walker, *American Shelter: An Illustrated Encyclopedia of the American Home* (Woodstock, NY, 1981), John Milnes Baker, *American House Styles: A Concise Guide* (New York, 1994), Gerald Foster, *American Houses: A Field Guide to the Architecture of the Home* (New York, 2004), and McAlester and McAlester, *A Field Guide to American Houses*.

13. Abbott Cummings, *The Framed Houses of Massachusetts Bay, 1625–1715,* and Dell Upton, "Vernacular Domestic Architecture in Eighteenth-Century Virginia," in *Winterthur Portfolio* 17, nos. 2–3 (Summer–Autumn 1982): 95–119. The earliest American Colonial and early National period house-plan typologies include Norman Morrison Isham and Albert F. Brown, *Early Rhode Island Houses* (Providence, RI, 1895), and Norman Morrison Isham and Albert F. Brown, *Early Connecticut Houses* (Providence, RI, 1900), 6–11. Many East Coast, regional architecture studies, such as Thomas C. Hubka, *Big House, Little House, Back House, Barn: The Connected Farm Buildings of New England* (Hanover, NH, 1984), 32–50, contain floor-plan development typologies.

14. For example, *Ordering Space: Types in Architecture and Design,* ed. Karen A. Franck and Lynda H. Schneekloth (New York, 1994).

15. Significant current efforts to address housing classification including plan analysis include Gottfried and Jennings, *American Vernacular Buildings and Interiors*; Christine Hunter, *Ranches, Rowhouses, and Railroad Flats* (New York, 1999); Daniel D. Reiff, *Houses from Books: Treatises, Pattern Books, and Catalogs in American Architecture, 1738–1950* (University Park, PA, 2000); Gowans, *The Comfortable House*; Jakle, Bastian, and Meyer, *Common Houses in America's Small Towns*; Virginia and Lee McAlester, *A Field Guide to American Houses*; Peter G. Rowe, *Making a Middle Landscape* (Cambridge, MA, 1991); Walker, *American Shelter*; and Foster, *American Houses*. Books that interpret and classify the broadest range of America's common houses as attempted in this book include Hunter, *Ranches, Rowhouses, and Railroad Flats*; Reiff, *Houses from Books*; Gottfried and Jennings, *American Vernacular Buildings and Interiors*; Gowans, *The Comfortable House*; Jakle, Bastian, and Meyer, *Common Houses in America's Small Towns*; Rowe, *Making a Middle Landscape*; Walker, *American Shelter*; Foster, *American Houses*; Baker, *American House Styles*; and McAlester and McAlester, *A Field Guide to American Houses*. Of these works, the perceptive studies of Hunter; Jakle, Bastian, and Meyer; and Reiff come closest to the inclusive goals of this book.

16. Various other works interpret the common aspects of everyday and domestic life from a different perspective, including Michel de Certeau, Luce Giard, and Pierre Mayol, *The Practice of Everyday Life* (Minneapolis, 1998), vol. 2: 251–56; Tony Judt, *Ill Fares the Land* (New

York, 2010), 21–25; Deirdre N. McCloskey, *The Bourgeois Virtues* (Chicago, 2006), 1–90; Witold Rybczynski, *Home: A Short History of an Idea* (New York, 1986); Henri Lefebvre, *A Critique of Everyday Life,* trans. John Moore (London, 1991); and Henry H. Glassie, *Passing the Time in Ballymenone: Culture and History of an Ulster Community* (Bloomington, IN, 1995).

17. The early critique of the suburbs was led by architecture and planning professions, as with Lewis Mumford, *The City in History* (New York, 1961), 486, and throughout; Vincent J. Scully, *American Architecture and Urbanism* (New York, 1969), 165, and throughout; and more recently by books such as James Howard Kunstler, *The Geography of Nowhere: The Rise and Decline of America's Man-Made Landscape* (New York, 1993). An early exception to this condemnation was Herbert Gans, *The Levittowners* (New York, 1967), as continued in Rosalyn Baxandall and Elizabeth Ewen, *Picture Window: How the Suburbs Happened* (New York, 2000), 158–67. Typical recent reassessments include *Second Suburb,* ed. Harris, as summarized in the foreword by Dell Upton.

18. Bigott, *From Cottage to Bungalow.* The general critique of many housing studies, such as *The Arts and the American Home, 1890–1930,* ed. Jessica H. Foy and Karal Ann Marling (Knoxville, TN, 1994); *American Home Life, 1880–1930,* ed. Jessica H. Foy and Thomas J. Schlereth (Knoxville, TN, 1992), and Gwendolyn Wright, *Building the Dream: A Social History of Housing in America* (Cambridge, MA, 1983), 154–76, is directed at the tendency to address all housing, including a large volume of working-class housing, based on research and ideas primarily derived from the study of upper-middle-class houses and families. This scholarship is not incorrect, except that it many cases it should not have been applied to the majority of middle- to working-class houses and families. While only a slip of emphasis in elite literature, it produces serious errors of interpretation for common housing studies.

19. This difficult-to-test assertion about the fluid origins of most vernacular house types cannot be proven here except to emphasize that there no widely recognized claims to specific sources or origin houses for most common vernacular houses. Historical studies do hint at evolutionary models for vernacular architectural development from earlier and primitive sources. This longing for origins is summarized by Joseph Rykwert, *On Adam's House in Paradise: The Idea of the Primitive Hut*

in *Architecture History* (Cambridge, MA, 1981). Unfortunately, similar mythic explanations have little or no relationship to the actual historic evolution of most vernacular houses.

20. The rebuttal to each of these four commonly held perceptions would each require extended analysis and is beyond the scope of this book. For example, the total numbers of kit-built common houses (Sears houses plus all other manufacturers) never exceeded .01 percent of the total number of houses produced for any year during the first half of the twentieth century, and often it was much less; see Doan, *American Housing Production, 1800–2000,* 21. In other words, although a relatively glamorous and easy-to-research topic, these houses are vastly overemphasized in the housing literature. (The same issues apply to owner-built houses, but the topic is extremely difficult to research.) Over a fifteen-year period in hundreds of survey neighborhoods from throughout the country, none of these four myths about house building was recorded in sufficient numbers to warrant reference in this book.

21. The theory of house shrinkage is articulated most succinctly by Wright, *Building the Dream,* 171 and throughout 154–76. Similar interpretations are repeated in many works, such as Sandy Isenstadt's "The Small House Era" in *The Modern American House* (Cambridge, UK, 2006), 14–58. In no analysis of the working- to middle-class housing literature reviewed for this book has this general theory of spatial reduction been cited, much less verified. Whether any significant percentage of upper-class families actually experienced real spatial reduction is a debatable topic which reflects the ideological concerns of an upper class and not an actual reduction in space. In any case, during the first half of the twentieth century, for a vast majority of Americans who left small unimproved houses for slightly larger and vastly improved houses, there was no shrinkage of house size, only modest but significant improvement and expansion. This assertion is confirmed, for example, in hundreds of Milwaukee case studies in research for this book.

22. Today multi-unit housing accounts for approximately one-third of housing units (U.S. Census Bureau, "American Housing Survey for the United States: 2005"), but until 1945 less than half of American households owned their own homes, and this percentage diminishes in earlier periods (Doan, *American Housing Production, 1880–2000,* 51).

23. This general critique of historic-preservation guidelines and nominating criteria is based on twelve years of service on Wisconsin's State Historic Preservation Board, where I observed at first hand the difficulties of awarding historic status to vernacular properties and environments.

24. For an excellent summary review of the issues of class in American society, see Margo Anderson, "The Language of Class in Twentieth-Century America," in *Social Science History* 12, no. 4 (Winter 1988): 349–75. Many authors fail to identify the basic demographics of housing class (particularly factors of wealth) and consequently misinterpret how the percentages of families in each class change between periods. For example, there is a dominant tendency to describe the majority population of late-nineteenth and early twentieth-century working-class Americans from a perspective of the middle to upper class. This standard mode of housing analysis is unfortunately supported by housing research that overwhelmingly documented either an upper middle class or an impoverished lower working class and consistently fail to adequately address a numerical majority of citizens living in common houses who fall between these two well-documented extremes. Although not usually emphasized in architectural literature, the dominance of English housing and domestic traditions and the English cultural aspirations of many Americans probably contributed to reinforcing a more exclusive English use of the term *middle class* in referring to an even smaller, more elite segment of the population, a wealthy merchant (middle) class that emerged in competition with an older aristocracy. For a view of English "middle class" traditions in American domestic development, see John Archer, *Architecture and Suburbia: From English Villa to American Dream, 1690–2000* (Minneapolis, 2005), 173–248.

2. Underlying Themes for Understanding Common Houses

1. Henry Glassie, *Folk Housing in Middle Virginia* (Knoxville, TN, 1975), 42.

2. My methods for common housing documentation and field survey span forty years, beginning with student neighborhood surveys in Eu-

gene, Oregon; Boston; and Milwaukee, and continuing in detailed housing studies primarily in Maine, Wisconsin, and Oregon. Over the last fifteen years, I have conducted detailed neighborhood case studies of the dominant forms of common housing within twenty-six metropolitan and rural areas throughout the country. (See chapter 2, note 13). Chapter 4 gives a summary of survey techniques for beginning a study of common houses. For standard methods of vernacular housing documentation and survey methods, see Carter and Cromley, *Invitation to Vernacular Architecture.*

3. The pattern of focusing on a few surviving, upper-class, early period houses as the focus of a region's early housing history, instead of focusing on more numerous smaller common houses, is, unfortunately well established throughout the country. For example, see a collection of Oregon's early settlement scholarship in Thomas Vaughan, ed., *Space, Style, and Structure: Building in Northwest America,* 2 vols. (Portland, OR, 1974).

4. For example, David L. Ames and Linda Flint McClelland, *National Register Bulletin: Historic Residential Suburbs* (Washington DC, 2002).

5. Prototype theory as defined in Eleanor Rosch et al., "Basic Objects in Natural Categories," *Cognitive Psychology* 8, no. 3 (July 1976): 382–439. Also see Ronald Langacker, *Foundations of Cognitive Grammar,* 2 vols. (Stanford, CA, 1987–91).

6. Glassie, *Folk Housing in Middle Virginia,* 13–18; Alison K. Hoagland, *Mine Towns: Buildings for Workers in Michigan's Copper Country* (Minneapolis, 2010), 1–54 and throughout.

7. See chapter 1, notes 4 and 5.

8. Thomas C. Hubka, "Just Folks Designing: Vernacular Designers and the Generation of Form," *Common Places,* ed. Dell Upton and John Michael Vlach (Athens, GA, 1986), 426–32. Henry Glassie has analyzed the vernacular methods of pre-modern vernacular designers in many works, most notably *Folk Housing in Middle Virginia,* 19–40 and throughout, and *Passing the Time in Ballymenone,* 315–424. For an overview of vernacular methods, see Carter and Cromley, *Invitation to Vernacular Architecture,* 13–18. Howard Davis provides an excellent analysis of the design decision-making context for common buildings in "Rules and

Knowledge about Building," in *The Culture of Building,* 85–218. Amos Rapoport provides a classic interpretation of environmental design in pre-modern societies in *House Form and Culture,* 18–45, 104–25.

9. Major studies of the bungalow include Clay Lancaster, *The American Bungalow, 1880–1930* (New York, 1985); Robert Winter, *The California Bungalow* (Los Angeles, 1980), and Anthony D. King, *The Bungalow* (New York, 1995), 127–55. Lancaster has a short chapter on the "box bungalow," a small, contractor-built house, but he does not analyze the term (*The American Bungalow,* 181–98). Generally, while these classic sources include pictures of common bungalows, the emphasis is clearly directed toward upper-class models, and there is little discussion of the contribution of common builders in the evolution of the most common forms of the bungalow. For a detailed analysis of this relationship, see Bigott, *From Cottage to Bungalow,* 19–53; Janet Ore, *The Seattle Bungalow: People and Houses, 1900–1940* (Seattle, 2007), 52–95; and Anna Andrzejewski, *One Builder: Marshall Erdman and Postwar Building and Real Estate Development in Madison, Wisconsin* (in press).

10. The total contribution of local builder-developers is outlined in a variety of different sources, including Warner, *Streetcar Suburbs,* 67–116; Keating, *Building Chicago,* 70–88; Weiss, *The Rise of the Community Builders,* 1–90; Hayward, *Baltimore's Alley Houses*; Rilling, *Making Houses*; and Carolyn S. Loeb, *Entrepreneurial Vernacular: Developers' Subdivisions in the 1920s* (Baltimore, 2001).

11. The literature about vernacular builders and construction is dominated by pre-modern, pre-industrial, pre–Civil War era studies—for example, Bishir, "Jacob W. Holt," 1–31; Garrison, *Two Carpenters*; and Glassie, *Folk Housing in Middle Virginia*. The changing nature of early industrialized building practices can be discerned from Rilling, *Making Houses*. Insights into the construction methods of "anonymous" common-house builders can be found in Hayward, *Baltimore's Alley Houses*; Warner, *Street Car Suburbs*; and Bigott, *From Cottage to Bungalow*. For a rare case study analysis of the complete developmental process behind the production of a recent upper-middle-class developer subdivision, see Witold Rybczynski, *Last Harvest: How a Cornfield Became New Daleville* (New York, 2007). Also see chapter 1, note 4.

12. These local variants are clearly evident, for example, in Thomas Carter and Peter Goss, *Utah's Historic Architecture, 1847–1940* (Salt Lake City, 1988).

13. The research methods for documenting the common houses of Buffalo, Pittsburgh, and Cincinnati were typical for the twenty-six metropolitan-area case studies I have made over the last fifteen years. Typically I made two three-to-five-day study tours of each area. Visitation was always preceded by months of preliminary research and the establishment of all-important local research contacts to facilitate neighborhood surveys and housing documentation. During visits, neighborhood reconnaissance with knowledgeable local experts guided my identification of the dominant forms of common housing in historic periods. A census analysis of house plan types would then be conducted, usually involving several neighborhoods from throughout a city or region, to obtain both dominant types in successive historic periods and a listing of the full range of local types. Survey estimates were followed by house visitation and the photo documentation and measurement of the each of the most dominant local types. Subsequent visits would test initial hypotheses and interview local historians and housing experts. Follow-up lectures would be given to neighborhood groups, schools, and historical societies in order to test initial theories and to "give back" to the local community.

14. There does not seem to be a consistent, uniform relationship between the influence of national house types and the particular local expression of these types. (In other words, it is highly variable.) This relationship between national and local (or high-style and vernacular) has similarities to the difficult-to-gauge influences of national pattern books on subsequent local and regional housing development. This challenging topic is examined by Kingston Heath in *Vernacular Architecture and Regional Design*; Howard Davis addresses this relationship as "tradition and innovation" in building form in *The Culture of Building*, 131–58.

3. Emphasizing the Floor Plan in Common Houses

1. Analysis of Milwaukee's common housing is based on fieldwork in Milwaukee and its suburban communities over twenty-five years. This research includes architecture studios and neighborhood association

projects—for example, housing documentation and lectures, and research studies of Milwaukee's housing co-authored with Professor Judith T. Kenny, Department of Geography, University of Wisconsin–Milwaukee. Co-authored articles include "Surveying Milwaukee's Residential Landscapes: Prospects for Research," in *The History of Milwaukee,* ed. Margo Anderson and Victor Greene (Urbana, IL, 2009); "Examining the American Dream: Housing Standards and the Emergence of a National Housing Culture, 1900–1930," in *Perspectives in Vernacular Architecture* 13, no. 1 (2006); and "The Transformation of the Workers' Cottage in Milwaukee's Polish Community," in *Perspectives in Vernacular Architecture, VIII,* ed. Sally McMurry and Ann Marie Adams (Knoxville, TN, 2000).

2. During the last six years, I have surveyed houses in most of Portland's neighborhoods and in fifteen towns throughout Oregon. I am currently assisting the Buckman neighborhood and the Architecture Heritage Center with a historic district nomination.

3. Gottfried and Jennings, *American Vernacular Buildings and Interiors, 1870–1960,* is a rare work of housing scholarship to recognize and emphasize the importance of plan and facade interchangeability during the late nineteenth century.

4. This study is based on survey and case-study housing research in the metropolitan areas of: Atlanta; Baton Rouge; Boston; Chicago; Cincinnati; Cleveland; Indianapolis; Los Angeles; Milwaukee; New York; Omaha; Pittsburgh; Portland, ME; Portland, OR; San Francisco; Seattle; Washington, DC; and Worcester; and small town and rural areas of Oregon, Wisconsin, Maine, Central Pennsylvania, Central New Jersey, New Hampshire, Central Montana, and Eastern Massachusetts. See chapter 2, note 13 for research and survey techniques.

5. See chapter 2, note 9.

6. See chapter 1, note 14, for the problems of current style-based and elite-oriented housing classification systems to address common vernacular-housing environments. For architectural histories of housing that primarily use architectural style and exterior form to classify housing, see Walker, *American Shelter*; David P. Handlin, *The American Home: Architecture and Society, 1815–1915* (Boston, 1979); Foster, *American Houses*; and McAlester and McAlester, *A Field Guide to American Houses.* Gwendolyn Wright skillfully analyzes the tendency of historians to appreciate historic

vernacular environments while simultaneously rejecting current equivalent vernacular environments in "On Modern Vernaculars and J. B. Jackson," in *Everyday America: Cultural Landscape Studies after J. B. Jackson,* ed. Chris Wilson and Paul Erling Groth (Berkeley, CA, 2003), 163–77.

7. The meaning of Louis Sullivan's expression "Form follows function" has been defined and redefined by architectural historians and critics. For Sullivan's early usage, see Martha Pollak, "Sullivan and the Orders of Architecture," in *Chicago Architecture, 1872–1922,* ed. John Zukowsky (Chicago, 1987), 260–64. For a summary of methods of floor-plan analysis to inform vernacular studies see "Invitation to the House on Richmond Avenue in Buffalo," in Carter and Cromley, *Invitation to Vernacular Architecture,* 83–95.

8. Henry Glassie has frequently emphasized the primacy of plan and the subordination of exterior expression in vernacular architecture, as in "Artifact and Culture, Architecture and Society," in *American Material Culture and Folklore,* ed. Simon Bronner (Ann Arbor, MI, 1985), 53. Howard Davis summaries the complexities of architectural and spatial usage in *The Culture of Building,* 3–21.

9. And the subject of my next book. For an assessment of how this transformation was typically accomplished by working-to middle-class families in common houses, see Joseph Biggott, *From Cottage to Bungalow;* Hoagland, *Mine Towns,* and Hubka and Kenny, "Examining the American Dream."

INDEX

Page numbers in *italics* refer to illustrations.

apartment, 2
architectural style naming, 2, 16–22
Arts-and-Crafts, *17*

box-ranch, *43*, 84
builders and speculative building process, 37–40, *38*
bungalow, *1*, 2, *2*, *8*, 38–39, *39*, *48*, *78*, *92*
bungalow plan types, *57*

Cape Cod, 2, *8*, *9*,*19*, *78*
census method naming, 31–37, *32*
center-chimney Cape Cod, *18*
chimneys, 79
Colonial, 2
Colonial-Revival, *19*
common home statistics, 2
composition-decomposition process, 37–38, *38*
corner-bay up-and-down duplex, *44*
current naming practices and sources, 10–14, *13*
current stylistic names, 11

difficult-to-identify houses, 4–6, 80–81
dominant common house plans (1800-2000), 52–63, *53–61*
doors, 79
duplex, 2, *44*, *80*
Dutch Colonial, *19*

early modern prototypes (1890-1950), *57–58*
elite housing focus limitations, 22–23
English, *49*
evolution mythology, 26
exterior observation for floor plan identification, 74–81
    chimneys, 79
    difficult-to-identify houses, 80–81
    doors, 79
    duplexes and multi-unit houses, 79–80
    kitchen location, 74–76, *75*
    personal artifacts, 79

exterior observation for floor plan identification (cont.)
    utilities, 79
    windows, 76–78, *77*, *78*
exterior shape, form, or massing names, 19–20

fieldwork techniques for floor plan identification, 72–74
flat, *2*
floor plan (v. facade) naming, 47–63, *48*, *51*
floor plan identification techniques, 69–81
    exterior observation for floor plan identification, 74–81
    fieldwork techniques, 72–74
    rules, 70–71
floor plan names, 20–22
four-square, *2*, *20*, *44*
four-square plan types, *57*

gable-over-porch, *20*, *44*
garage-in-front ranch, *43*
Georgian form, I house, *18*
Gothic style, side gable, *17*

historic naming trends, 16–22
home ownership mythology, 28

I-house, *21*
Italianate, *2*

kitchen location, 74–76, *75*

local/regional preferences and national housing types, 40–45, *42*, *43*, *44*

manufactured home plan types, *61*
McMansion, 23, *24*
minimal-traditional, *49*, 89
Modern Colonial, *19*
myths and misconceptions, 22–29

naming problems, 1–6, 10–15
naming system recommendation/suggestion
    See two-part common home identification method
narrow-lot ranch, *43*
national housing types and local/regional preferences, 40–45, *42*, *43*, *44*
neo-classical, *18*

one-room plan types, *53*
origin mythology, 26

parlor-by-pass plan types, *42, 48, 55*
pattern interpretation, 88–93
    constraints context, 88–89, *89*
    egalitarian principles, 92–93
    increments of change, 91–92, *91*
    repetition and conformity, 89–91, *90*
period-revival and minimal-traditional plan types, *58*
period-revival style, *49*
permanence mythology, 28–29
personal artifacts, 79
plan prototypes (1800-2000), *53–61*
plans
    advantages (over façade basis) for naming, 50–52
    difficult-to-identify houses, 4–6, 80–81
    dominant plans by era, 53–61
    exterior examination fieldwork techniques, 72–74
    exterior examination introduction, 69–70
    exterior examination rules for naming, 70–71, 74–81
    as naming system basis, 20–22
    pattern interpretation characteristics, 88–94
    prototypes, 53–61
    room function and usage naming, 63–68, *65–68*
plan types by era, 52–63, *53–61*
    1800-1860 plan types, *53–54*
    1820-1900 plan types, *55–56*
    1890-1950 plan types, *57–58*
    1940-2000 plan types, *59–61*
Polish flat, *9, 28, 48*
popular common house plans, 52–63, *53–61*
Prairie, *17*
pre-modern prototypes (1800-1860), *53–54*
professional evaluation of naming practices, 14–15
prototype naming, 35–37
pyramid, *20, 21*

Queen Anne, 2, *17*

ranch, 2, *8, 43, 70, 83–87*
ranch plan types, *59*
recommended naming system
    See two-part common home identification method
room function and usage naming, 63–68, *65–68*

shotgun, *2, 21*
shrinking house misconception, 27
side-entry, turn-of-the-century, *20*

side-gable plan types, *55*
side-hall plan types, *54*
side-hall plan with rear additions, *91*
side-hall row house, *9*
single-family misconception, 28
social class naming limitations, 22–23
speculative building and builder mythology, 26–27
split-level, 2, *2*
split-level plan types, *60*
standard ranch, *43*
statistics, 2, 7
style naming, 2, 16–22
suburban minimal-traditional plan types, *61*
suburbia mythology, 23–24
suggested naming system
    See two-part common home identification method

telescope, *42*
terminology explanation, 6–10
transitional prototypes (1820-1900), *55–56*
trickle-down mythology, 24–25
Tudor, *17*, *49*
two-part common home identification method, 83–93
    historical and cultural pattern discernment, 89–95
    overview, 83
    strategies for starting, 83–88
two-room and one-deep plan types, *54*
two-up, two-down, *42*, *90*

uncommon homes, 7, *7*, 8
utilities, 79

vernacular names, 2
Victorian, *17*
Victorian house/expanded side-hall plan types, *56*

windows, 76–78, *77*, *78*

HOUSES WITHOUT NAMES was designed and typeset on a Macintosh computer system using InDesign software. The body text is set in 9.5/16 Mercury and display type is set in Helvetica Neue. This book was designed and typeset by Chad Pelton.

www.ingramcontent.com/pod-product-compliance
Lightning Source LLC
Chambersburg PA
CBHW051352070526
44584CB00025B/3739